NOBODY WANTS TO READ YOUR SH*T

NOBODY WANTS TO READ YOUR SH*T

Why That Is and What You Can Do About It

STEVEN PRESSFIELD

BLACK IRISH ENTERTAINMENT, LLC

New York/Los Angeles

BLACK IRISH ENTERTAINMENT LLC
223 EGREMONT PLAIN ROAD
PMB 191
NORTH EGREMONT, MA 01230

COVER DESIGN BY DERICK TSAI, MAGNUS REX
COVER SAMPLER DESIGNED AND STITCHED BY JULIE JACKSON
@SUBVERSIVECROSSSTITCH.COM
EDITING BY SHAWN COYNE

FIRST BLACK IRISH ENTERTAINMENT EDITION
MAY 2016

FOR INFORMATION ABOUT SPECIAL DISCOUNTS
FOR BULK PURCHASES, VISIT WWW.BLACKIRISHBOOKS.COM

ISBN: 978-1936891-49-8
EBOOK ISBN: 978-936891-50-4

1 2 3 4 5 6 7 8 9 10

NOBODY WANTS TO READ YOUR SH*T

1.

THE MOST IMPORTANT LESSON I EVER LEARNED

In a long career as a writer, you find yourself working in a number of different disciplines. Each one teaches its own lessons. Not surprisingly, many carry over from one field to another. What you learn writing movies helps you when you move on to novels, and what you pick up writing fiction proves invaluable when you turn to nonfiction.

My first writing job was in the field I hated most and respected least—advertising. Yet the ad biz taught me the most, and it was stuff that served me powerfully in every subsequent incarnation.

Next I tried novels but I learned practically nothing because I was alone and kept making the same mistakes over and over. It wasn't until I got to Hollywood and began writing for the movies that I really started to understand what a story was. So when I went back to novels after that, I had a sound foundation in narrative structure—what makes a story work and what makes it not work.

Moving into nonfiction taught further lessons, but not the ones I expected. And writing self-help took me into a whole other arena that to my non-surprise was at least as much about narrative as it was about content.

But of everything I learned, the most important lesson came at the beginning, on the very first day of my very first job. The lesson was, "Nobody wants to read your shit." (See chapter 4.)

2.

MY FAMILY

There were no artists in my family. Everyone was in business. My dad wore a suit and went to work in an office. So did all my uncles and all my mother and father's friends. Now that I think about it, there were no artists in my entire hometown/high school/universe.

My friend Brad Holliday's dad was a magazine illustrator. If you went over to Brad's house at two in the afternoon, his old man was just stumbling downstairs from his attic office, barefoot, unshaven, in his pajamas.

Growing up, that was my idea of what an artist was.

It was pretty fucking appalling.

3.

A WRITING JOB

I got a job at Benton & Bowles in New York City. B&B was a big advertising agency with offices in the Tishman Building at 666 Fifth Avenue. The year was 1967. I was a twenty-three-year-old junior copywriter making $150 a week. The accounts I worked on were Squibb, Gravy Train dog food, and Chemical New York, a bank.

Benton & Bowles had ten or twelve floors in the building. I remember the first morning riding the elevator up to the office. The lighted panel above the doors said:

ACCOUNT MANAGEMENT DEPT	18th Floor
ACCOUNT MANAGEMENT DEPT	17th Floor
CREATIVE DEPT	16th Floor
CREATIVE DEPT	15th Floor
MEDIA DEPT	14th Floor
RESEARCH DEPT	12th Floor

What made my heart beat faster were those two magic words: Creative Department.

That was me.

I was "creative."

This was the first time in my life that that idea had occurred to me.

4.

NOBODY WANTS
TO READ YOUR SH*T

The first thing you learn in advertising is that no one wants to read your shit.

Your ads, I mean.

People hate ads. I hate them myself. I hate TV commercials. Why should I waste my valuable time watching that lying garbage, trying to sell me crap I don't need or want?

Sometimes young writers acquire the idea from their years in school that the world is waiting to read what they've written. They get this idea because their teachers had to read their essays or term papers or dissertations.

In the real world, no one is waiting to read what you've written.

Sight unseen, they hate what you've written. Why? Because they might have to actually read it.

Nobody wants to read anything.

Let me repeat that. Nobody—not even your dog or your mother—has the slightest interest in your commercial for Rice Krispies or Delco batteries or Preparation H. Nor does anybody care about your one-act play, your Facebook page or your new sesame chicken joint at Canal and Tchoupitoulas.

It isn't that people are mean or cruel. They're just busy.

Nobody wants to read your shit.

What's the answer?

1) Streamline your message. Focus it and pare it down to its simplest, clearest, easiest-to-understand form.

2) Make its expression fun. Or sexy or interesting or scary or informative. Make it so compelling that a person would have to be crazy NOT to read it.

3) Apply that to all forms of writing or art or commerce.

When you understand that nobody wants to read your shit, your mind becomes powerfully concentrated. You begin to understand that writing/reading is, above all, a transaction. The reader donates his time and attention, which are supremely valuable commodities. In return, you the writer must give him something worthy of his gift to you.

When you understand that nobody wants to read your shit, you develop empathy.

You acquire the skill that is indispensable to all artists and entrepreneurs—the ability to switch back and forth in your imagination from your own point of view as writer/painter/seller to the point of view of your reader/gallery-goer/customer. You learn to ask yourself with every sentence and every phrase: Is this interesting? Is it fun or challenging or inventive? Am I giving the reader enough? Is she bored? Is she following where I want to lead her?

5.

SOMETIMES YOU GOTTA BE SOMEBODY'S SLAVE

I got to Hollywood in the early '80s, during the heyday of the "spec script." This was a great time to be a screen-writer. Not necessarily for me though. I spent my first five years specking scripts—nine of them, six months of work for each.

None of them sold.

I had an agent at the time named Mike Werner. Mike believed in me but he was getting tired of taking my specs out to the town and watching them die.

One day he said, "Steve, how would you like to team up with another writer? An established writer."

Mike had another client, whom I'll call Stanley, who had been the force behind two huge hits.

"I know you want to do your own stuff," Mike said. "But working with Stan, at least you'll be in play. You'll make money and your work will get produced."

I said yes.

Stan and I worked together for five years.

You have to take a lot of blows, being the junior mem-ber of a working team. But, as Mike said, you are now in play.

You have a seat at the table.

6.

"I'LL BE OVER
AT NINE THIRTY"

When Stan and I started working together, he said, "Let's work at your house. I'll come over at nine thirty and we'll start."

The first day Stan showed up at 12:30.

Next day: 1:30.

This went on for a month. I kept saying, "Stanley, I'm sitting here doing nothing! What's the problem? Why can't you get here on time?"

But six weeks into our partnership, Stan was still arriving mid-afternoon. We'd work for a desultory hour, then be so exhausted and dispirited we'd have to quit.

Finally one morning I said to myself, "Steve, just start. Don't wait for Stan."

When Stan arrived that day at one thirty, I had seven pages to show him. We went over the work. Stan had a bunch of smart things to say. We tweaked the pages, made plans for the next day's work, and then Stan went home.

The next day I had six more pages. We did more good work.

I began to realize that this is what Stan had wanted all along. He was not really a writer-writer. He was a producer-writer. He needed a partner who was a writer-writer.

Stan got us work. In meetings, he did all the talking. Stan was a little nutty, but studios and production entities were hot to work with him. He had delivered two big hits. He was a brand.

Writing with Stan, for the first time in my life I was making enough money to actually survive.

(8)

7.

"STEVE, YOUR EGO IS GETTING OUT OF HAND"

Four years into our partnership, I began agitating for more credit. Stan wouldn't give it to me.

We had a mutual friend named Gregory, who managed writers and directors. One day Gregory said to me, "Steve, lemme take you for a cup of coffee."

We drove to a deli called Brent's in the valley.

"Steve," Gregory began, "you're a good guy and I like you, but your ego is getting out of hand. I want to talk to you before you wind up doing something you'll regret."

The waitress came with Gregory's Reuben and my pastrami on rye. Around the deli, booths were populated with other Hollywood one-on-one confabs just like ours. Gregory waited until the waitress had set down our plates and departed.

Gregory said he knew I was frustrated. He could see that I felt I was doing all the work and getting none of the credit. He understood that, he said. He didn't blame me for feeling that way.

Gregory cited three or four screenwriting teams that I was familiar with, two-man teams that were getting work and getting movies made. One I'll call Mike and Jim. In fact Mike was sitting at another booth in Brent's Deli right now, by himself, going over some notes.

"Steve, everybody in town knows Mike does all the work in that team. Jim doesn't even live here. He's in Madison, Wisconsin, for Christ's sake. He doesn't get into town two times a year!"

But, Gregory said, Jim has the name. Jim has had hits on his own. Jim is the star. Mike does the writing, but Jim brings in the jobs.

Gregory was telling me that if I kept agitating with Stanley for more credit, I'd kill the golden goose. He advised me to open my eyes and take a realistic view of my position.

"Steve, you could have the script for *Gone with the Wind* under your arm, written by you alone. You could take it to every studio in town. You know what would happen?"

I knew.

"But if you took that same script into those same studios, written by Stan and you, you'd be cashing a check for seven figures.

"Stan is the brand," Gregory continued. "He's had hits. Stan's name gets you the meetings. His reputation gets you the work.

"Stan has had two partners before you, Steve, and he's had hits with both of them. Do you know what that means in this town? It means Stan is perceived as the key element. He's the variable that consistently produces success."

Gregory could see he was getting through to me. My pastrami sandwich was sitting untouched.

"Steve, I understand your frustration, and you're right to feel frustrated. You *are* busting your ass and you *are* doing terrific work. But Stan has had hits with partners before you and he'll have hits with partners after you. The bottom line is this:

"If you want real credit, you have to write a script on your own and have a hit on your own."

8.

TWO FUNDAMENTAL TRUTHS

Have you reckoned the two principles in these first few pages?

1) Nobody wants to read your shit.
2) If you want to write and be recognized, you have to do it yourself.

From these twain, all else proceeds.

BOOK ONE

ADVERTISING

9.

IT'S HARD TO WRITE AN AD

I was never worth a damn at writing ads. It's hard. You gotta be great.

But the training is sensational.

Like being a lawyer or a journalist or a prostitute, being an ad person teaches you a very specific way of thinking. That way has been indispensable to me in the fields I have later entered—the writing of movies, fiction, nonfiction, even self-help.

The following sixteen chapters list lessons that every Mad Man (and Mad Woman) learns.

10.

DON'T THINK IN ADS, THINK IN CAMPAIGNS

There's a phrase in advertising: "pool-outs." It's related to "spin-offs" in TV.

What it means is that from a single campaign concept, if it's strong enough, can come dozens of individual ads and commercials (also known as "executions.") Each one works as part of the broader concept and each one reinforces the overall theme.

How big is your concept?

Answer: How many pool-outs will it spawn?

Nike started with Michael Jordan and the Air Jordan shoe. The concept was "Buy Nike and you will Be Like Mike." That was 1984. The concept still drives every ad and TV spot that Nike runs (although now it's powered by Serena and LeBron and Rory McIlroy).

Same concept, different executions.

11.

THINKING IN CONCEPTS

Because everyone hates to read ads or watch TV commercials ("Nobody Wants to Read Your Sh*t"), the ad writer must come up with some ingenious way of making her material irresistible.

It isn't enough to catch the reader's eye. You can do that with cute kittens or a wet T-shirt.

You also have to sell the product. There must be a message, and that message must stick. It must have meaning in terms of the product. It must make the reader/viewer think, "Hmm, that makes sense," or, "Hmm, I like that."

If you imagine this is easy, try it sometime.

12.

COME UP WITH A CONCEPT

What is a concept?

A concept, in advertising terms, is not just a mindless slogan like "Bring out the Best Foods and bring out the best." Nor is it a generic, baseless claim like "Gets dentures whiter."

A concept takes a conventional claim and puts a spin on it.

A concept establishes a frame of reference that is greater than the product itself.

A concept sets the product in a context that makes the viewer behold the product with fresh eyes—and perceive it in a positive, compelling light.

A concept frames (or, more frequently, re-frames) the issue entirely.

One of the seminal concepts in advertising history is Avis Rent a Car's "We're #2 so we try harder."

"We're #2 so we try harder" turns a negative ("We're second best and thus inferior") into a positive ("You'll get better service from us because we'll work our butts off to catch #1 Hertz") by making us look at the issue ("Which is the best company to rent a car from?") from a whole new angle.

Nike's sports-hero campaign is a concept.

De Beers' "A diamond is forever" is a concept.

"If you're not whitening, you're yellowing" is a concept.

 A good concept makes the audience see your product from a very specific, sympathetic point of view and by its

(18)

logic (or faux logic) renders all other points of view and all competing products moot and impotent.

Diamonds were once viewed as commodities. Why should I buy a diamond engagement ring? What's wrong with rubies or sapphires? But when ad makers serving their client De Beers—the South African mining company that controlled 90 percent of the world's diamond supply—came up with the concept of enlisting the indestructibility of a diamond ("the hardest material in the universe") as a symbol of everlasting love ... wow.

After "A diamond is forever," if you bought your fiancée any other kind of engagement ring, you were saying you didn't love her.

Concepts work in politics too.

"Death panels" is a concept.

"Job creators" is a concept.

"Pro-life" is a concept. So is "pro-choice."

A concept can be complete balderdash. It can be evil.

"The master race."

"Manifest destiny."

"Operation Iraqi Freedom."

When you as a writer carry over and apply this mode of thinking to other fields, say the writing of novels or movies or nonfiction, the first question you ask yourself at the start of any project is, "What's the concept?"

Every work of art, from the Sistine Chapel to the Golden Gate Bridge to the King James Bible, is founded on a concept.

A diet should have a concept.

An invasion of a foreign country should have a concept.

A salad should have a concept.

13.

FLASH FORWARD: CONCEPT IN MOVIES

The '80s in Tinseltown was the era of the "high-concept" movie. The seminal example was *Die Hard* starring Bruce Willis, from a novel by Roderick Thorp, screenplay by Jeb Stuart and Steven de Souza. Just as in advertising, *Die Hard* spawned not just a rash of sequels and prequels, but a slew of pool-outs.

Passenger 57 was *Die Hard* on an airplane.

Hard Rain was *Die Hard* in a hurricane.

Die Hard in jail? *Die Hard* on the moon? No problem. The concept is like a key. Insert, turn, it works.

What exactly is a high-concept movie?

A high-concept movie is a film 1) whose narrative idea can be communicated in ten seconds or less (in other words, the perfect sound bite for an ad or a word-of-mouth recommendation), and 2) as soon as you hear the idea, you can imagine all the cool scenes that are certain to be in the movie (and that you want to see).

> A gang of thieves takes over a high-rise office building at night, planning to steal the corporate fortune in the basement. What they don't know is that one rogue cop happens to be in the building.

As soon as you hear this idea, you see the entire movie. Bruce Willis fights the bad guys in an elevator shaft. He fights them on the rooftop. He exchanges wise-cracks with them. In the end he kills/captures them all.

I was in Hollywood during this era. As soon as I heard the idea of the high-concept movie, I knew exactly what it was. It was the Avis/Volkswagen/American Express campaigns, only done as motion pictures.

14.

FLASH FORWARD: CONCEPT IN LITERATURE

It sounds like I'm making fun of the idea of concept. I'm not. *Game of Thrones* is a concept. *Orange Is the New Black* is a concept. *The Walking Dead* is a concept.

Beethoven's *Ninth* is a concept.

Guernica is a concept.

Hamlet is a concept.

I believe absolutely in concepts.

At the inception of any project I ask myself, "What is the concept?"

I won't tackle anything until I know the concept.

Concept works for the loftiest literary stuff there is.

Consider Homer's *Iliad*. The subject matter of *The Iliad* is the Trojan War. The Trojan War lasted for ten years. Homer could have written the history of the whole damn thing if he had wanted.

But even in 900 B.C., great storytellers understood concept.

So instead of narrating a decade of repetitive and tedious material, the poet trimmed the onstage time of his tale to a few days in the middle of the war.

He came up with a concept:

The wrath of Achilles.

That's the theme of *The Iliad*. That's the hook. That's the controlling idea.

The Greeks' preeminent champion, Achilles—

an invincible warrior against whom no hero of the enemy can stand (and upon whom victory for the Greeks depends)—takes offense at an insult offered by the Greeks' king, Agamemnon.

In rage and pride, Achilles quits the fight. He lays down his spear and shield and takes a seat on the sidelines.

"Let my countrymen discover, by their suffering without me fighting as their champion, how by far the greatest of them I am."

This is high-concept. Don't laugh.

From this ten-second pitch, we can project the entire epic. We see the sub-fights, starring Hector, Odysseus, Ajax, Paris, Diomedes. We see the Greeks starting to lose. We see the Trojan champion, Hector, growing in stature and confidence. We see the battle swinging so far in the Trojans' favor that they have pinned the Greeks with their backs to the sea and are attacking their beached ships with torches and firebrands.

And we see Achilles, at the moment of supreme peril, charging to the rescue, defeating the Trojan champions and saving the day.

And because we're smart and savvy readers, we know also that, since Achilles' wrath represents the sin of pride, he (and his fellow Greeks) will have paid in oceans of blood before this final hour of victory—and that the victory itself, for the Greeks and for Achilles, will be at least half tragedy.

Sounds great, doesn't it?

15.

IT'S OKAY TO BE CREATIVE

In the '50s and early '60s, there was no such thing as a "creative person." Even in advertising there were no "creative people." Writers wore suits and ties like Jon Hamm in *Mad Men*.

That all changed in the mid-60s with the arrival of Bill Bernbach, George Lois, Helmut Krone, and a new generation of copywriters and art directors.

The writers were mostly Jews and the art directors mostly Italians. Prior to their advent, the ad biz had been the exclusive province of guys with last names like Ogilvy and Bates.

Overnight it became cool to be creative.

For me this was revolutionary. It was life changing. I remember sitting in meetings and looking around at the other weirdos, geeks, freaks, and ethno-barbarians.

I said to myself, "It's okay to be the kind of person I am."

It's okay to be anxious.

It's okay to be unable to sleep.

It's okay to lack self-esteem.

It's okay to be an introvert, to seek out the quiet corners at a cocktail party, to care about quality, to have your mood be affected by your surroundings.

My role-options in life and career, I realized, were not limited to Businessman, Athlete, and Boneheaded Patriot.

All of a sudden I understood why I was so moody, neurotic, simultaneously paranoid and megalomaniac, mistrustful, uneasy, driven by ambition but paralyzed by guilt about my ambition, horny, obsessive, compulsive, obsessive-compulsive, not to mention shy, withdrawn, and dandruff-ridden.

I was creative.

All creative people were like that!

16.

CLIENT'S DISEASE

If you've ever been in business, you've serviced clients. Maybe you've even been a client.

All clients have one thing in common:

They're in love with their product/company/service.

In the ad biz, this is called Client's Disease.

I have seen a thousand clients be presented with brilliant campaigns for their products or services and have them ruin these campaigns by loading them up with their own lame bullshit.

Watching this, I vowed that if I ever found myself in the position of being a client—even if it was something as mundane as hiring a designer to remodel my kitchen—I would shut up and let the professional do her work. I've been true to that pledge, and it has never failed.

What the ad person understands that the client does not is that nobody gives a damn about the client or his product.

You, the client, may be in love with your support undergarments. And your support undergarments may in fact be the best support undergarments in the world.

Nobody cares.

That's the reality of the battlefield you're waging war on.

What to do if you're a client?

Back off.

Shut up.

Call in the pros from Dover and let them do their magic.

The pros understand that nobody wants to read their shit. They will start from that premise and employ all their arts and all their skills to come up with some brilliant stroke that will cut through that indifference, that clutter, that B.S.

I have sat in a hundred meetings where ad people humored, cajoled, and flattered the client, as of course they must. "We love your new detergent/SUV/dentifrice!"

Then as soon as the client headed for the elevators and the doors closed behind him, the writers and art directors turned to one another and got down to business.

"Okay, how do we sell this piece of shit?"

17.

STEAL WITHOUT SHAME

In the ad biz, you work in two-man teams—a copywriter and an art director. One is responsible for the words, the other for the pictures.

The first art director I was ever paired with was a gentleman my father's age, a World War II infantry vet named Zoltan Medvecky. Med was a star, a prize-winning pro. He and I had been given an assignment to do an ad for the international division of Chemical Bank.

I was excited because it was the first time I had ever worked with someone who really knew what he was doing (as opposed to the other junior A.D.s I had until then been paired with.) I was primed to watch and learn.

Med said we should work in his office because it was five times bigger than my cubicle and it had a door.

We came up with a headline pretty quickly (actually Med came up with it) and a concept for the visual.

Then Med opened a huge flat file drawer and began poring through magazines and photography books. I asked him what he was doing.

"Stealing."

I was shocked. "Stealing? You can't do that!"

Med thumbed through a dozen books and mags until he came to a year-old issue of *LIFE*. "Ah," he said. He had stopped at an editorial piece—a page with one-third white space at the bottom, a single black-and-white grainy photo up top, and a one-line caption beneath the photo.

He stole that layout.

"But, Med, isn't that cheating?"

"This layout in *LIFE*," Med said, "is straight-up reporto-rial photojournalism. See? A war photo, with the figures underlit and the light source—the late afternoon sun—coming from one side, throwing the other side into dramatic shadow. See how gritty it looks? A real gravitas shot."

Med showed me how he had tweaked the layout and made it work as an ad. I had to admit, it looked great.

"We're taking the *LIFE* photographer's straight-up look and reconceiving it, borrowing the aspects that possess gravity—and that no one else has used in an ad—to reinforce the impression we want to convey, which implies real-world grit and competence in an overseas setting."

Med reached across and put his hand on my shoulder.

"Kid, it ain't stealing if you put a spin on it."

18.

ALL YOU DO ALL DAY
IS THINK

Advertising is great training for the movie industry and for writing novels and nonfiction because all you do all day is think.

That's your job.

Sit there and come up with ideas.

Sometimes people who have worked in other professions will attempt to make the switch to writing. They struggle at first because they've never spent all day living entirely inside their heads.

19.

HOW TO GET
A BAD IDEA

What's hard about advertising is that the job is not just to produce good ideas but to produce them on demand.

Mad Men got that right.

The working weekend. The all-nighter. But even in the normal flow of day-to-day assignments, you're working on demand.

It's easy to get a lousy idea on demand. It's not that hard to come up with a mediocre idea. But a good idea?

I worked in advertising off and on for seven to ten years. I don't know if I ever had a really good idea.

I learned a lot about having bad ideas, though.

When you try too hard, you have bad ideas.

When you work mechanically, you have bad ideas.

When you follow formula, you have bad ideas.

When you're desperate or panicky, you have bad ideas.

I learned that good writers and good art directors had good ideas over and over. And bad writers and bad art directors had bad ideas over and over.

I knew I had to figure out how to become one of the good writers.

20.

PROBLEMS AND SOLUTIONS

When an ad person comes up with an outstanding idea, she is congratulated with this phrase: "Great solution."

In advertising, you think of assignments as "problems." Your job is to come up with a solution.

Here's a typical problem:

Our client Samsung's smartphone is technically superior to Apple's iPhone 12, but Apple's hip/nerd/great design/Steve Jobs customer love affair is killing us. How can we turn the tables and make Samsung hip?

Or:

Our client, the American Poultry Association, sells six gazillion turkeys on Thanksgiving and none for the whole rest of the year. How can we make turkey into a year-round "go to" meat?

Problems seeking solutions. This is a very powerful way of thinking about the creative process.

Implicit in this point of view is the idea that the answer already exists within the question, that *the solution is embedded within the problem.*

If your job is to find that solution, the first step is to define the problem.

21.

DEFINING THE PROBLEM

In the ad biz, 20 percent of your time is taken up pursuing New Business. What this means is the agency going out and pitching new accounts.

Some accounts seem to be in play all the time. Burger King. 7Up. Chrysler.

To ask why these businesses are always in trouble (and always looking for new ad campaigns to save them) is to ask, "What is the problem?"

Answer—these companies are all perceived as losers.

They're second best, perennial bridesmaids and also-rans. Burger King is behind McDonald's, 7Up trails Coke, Chrysler lags behind Ford and GM.

When in 1967 some very smart people on the 7Up account at J. Walter Thompson came up with a campaign called "the Uncola," they solved the problem.

The problem wasn't taste. The problem wasn't price. The problem wasn't sugar content.

The problem was the public's perception of 7Up as a loser.

Calling 7Up "the Uncola" positioned the drink not as a poor second-best to Coke or Pepsi, but as an equal alternative. Just as good, only different.

Define the problem and you're halfway to the solution.

22.

FLASH FORWARD: DEFINING THE PROBLEM IN FICTION

When your novel or screenplay is disintegrating before your eyes, it is not a bad idea to fall back on thinking like an ad man.

Ask not, "What is the solution?"

Ask, "What is the problem?"

The problem in fiction, from the thrashing writer's point of view, is almost always, "What is this damn thing *about*?"

In other words, what's the theme?

What's the theme of our book, our play, our movie script? What's the theme of our new restaurant, our start-up, our video game?

When we don't know the theme, we don't know the Problem.

Do you remember the pilot for "Breaking Bad"?

In that first hour airing on January 20, 2008, Walter White gets hit with lot of stuff. He is diagnosed with inoperable cancer. To provide for his family after his death, he decides to start cooking methamphetamine. He teams up with a former student, sells his first batch, and along the way kills two competing criminals. Wow. How did Vince Gilligan, the show's creator, make all this stuff cohere? And how did he keep it together for six superb seasons?

The answer is in one scene in the pilot. The scene takes place in Walter White's high school chemistry class.

He asks the kids, "What is chemistry about?" Several students offer lame answers. Then our hero, played brilliantly by Bryan Cranston, answers the question himself.

> WALTER WHITE
> Change. Chemistry is the study of change.
> Elements combine and change into compounds. That's all of life, right? Solution, dissolution. Growth. Decay. Transformation. It's fascinating, really.

That speech is not there by accident. It is Vince Gilligan's statement of the theme.

Problem: What is this show about?
Solution: Transformation.

From this point in the series, from the pilot to the final season, every episode and every scene will be about transformation. When the writers become lost and feel their control over their material slipping away, they will return to this touchstone.

"Make this moment be about transformation."

And no one, of course, will transform more than our protagonist, mild-mannered Walter White.

23.

CALL TO ACTION

Every ad or commercial (or direct-mail piece or political flyer or FREE post in the PennySaver) ends with a "call to action."

Buy!

Subscribe!

Place your order now!

I hate those, don't you? But this single, extremely obvious principle (that was probably in practice back in Babylonia and a thousand years before that) may be the most important of all.

If you don't ask for the sale, how are you gonna get it?

The call to action is also, in storytelling terms, the "payoff."

It's Act Three

It's the climax.

We'll talk more about this when we get into movies, fiction, and nonfiction.

24.

ART IS ARTIFICE

I remember the first time I saw a script for a TV commercial.

There were the characters, there was the dialogue, there was the description of what action would happen.

I was dumbstruck.

You mean the actors don't just make up their lines on the spot? How can this be? It's all planned out? Where they stand? What they do? What they say?

I was tremendously disappointed and, at the same time, I felt terribly foolish. How could I not have known this? Of course there's a script. Of course it's all planned out in great detail.

Nothing is spontaneous. Everything is the product of deliberate conception, deliberate thought. Steve, you're an idiot to have this surprise you.

That was a big lesson and one that applied down the line in every other creative field.

Art is artifice.

25.

IT'S OKAY NOT TO BE 100% PURE

I worked in advertising three separate times, always to save up money to write a novel. Without that cash and that freedom, I would never have been able to pursue the work I loved.

And even though toiling in the Mad Ave trenches may have been selling out, working for the Man, prostituting one's talent etc., had I tried instead to be simon-pure and work on real writing only, my corpse would've been found in a cardboard shelter under a freeway overpass.

Ridley Scott worked in advertising. So did Satyajit Ray and Scott Fitzgerald and Salman Rushdie and hundreds of others who went on to produce immortal stuff in the real artistic world.

It's okay to work for Mr. Charley once in a while.

We can't all be Bob Dylan or Neil Young.

BOOK TWO

FICTION, PART ONE

26.

ROOTLESS

When I was twenty-four I quit advertising for the first time and set out to write a novel. I was no more prepared for embarking on such a passage than the typical twenty-four-year-old would be to march off to war or to jump off the top of the Empire State Building.

Four years later I was broke, divorced, etc., having in the interim crossed the United States thirteen times in my '65 Chevy van, supporting myself as, variously, a cab driver, bartender, substitute teacher, attendant in a mental hospital, a tractor-trailer driver, an oilfield roustabout, and a migratory fruit picker. The last straw came on a gale-scoured highway in November '72 in Amarillo, Texas, when a friend I had just made, a ranch hand who was traveling with his new wife and all their worldly goods in two paper bags, invited me to come with him to work cattle on his brother's spread east of Lubbock. For a few seconds I thought about it.

A cowboy.

Would that round out my American odyssey?

I passed and came home to New York where I found work again as an advertising copywriter.

27.

CLUELESS

I was twenty-nine when I quit advertising for the second time and, for the second time, set out to write a novel.

Here's what I did not know and had never heard of:

Genre.

Narrative device.

Theme.

Inciting incident.

Three-act (or multiple-act) structure.

Crisis, climax, resolution.

And everything else.

I had $2,700 in savings. I packed my Chevy van and moved from New York to Carmel Valley, California. I rented a small house behind a slightly larger house for $105 a month. I had my cat, Mo, a table, and my Smith-Corona typewriter.

I plunged in.

28.

MY DEMONS

I had no conception of Resistance in those days. I did not know that there existed inside my head an invisible, insidious, intractable, indefatigable force whose sole object was to keep me from doing my work, i.e., finishing the book I had been trying to write for seven years—and ultimately to destroy me, physically, psychologically, and spiritually.

All I knew was that I couldn't finish anything.

My pattern was to quit.

To fold.

To flake.

I'd get the ball all the way to the one-yard line. Then I'd bail.

That was my pattern.

That was what I always did.

That was the demon I was fighting in that little house behind the slightly bigger house.

Either I would slay that dragon or it would slay me.

29.

READING

There was a tiny branch library in Carmel Valley. I started taking out books. I took out every book that I should have read in college but didn't because I was too busy shooting pool and playing poker.

I read *War and Peace*. I read *Crime and Punishment*. I read *Fathers and Sons*. I read Stendhal's *The Red and the Black*; I read Knut Hamsun's *Hunger*. I read Proust and Balzac and Andre Malraux. I read *Madame Bovary*, I read *One Day in the Life of Ivan Denisovitch*, I read *All Quiet on the Western Front*. I read Joyce and Yeats and Dylan Thomas, Hemingway, Fitzgerald, Steinbeck, Henry Miller, Jack Kerouac, William Burroughs. I'd finish writing each day and pick up another timeless classic and submerge myself in it.

What did I learn?

Not a fucking thing.

I didn't even know there was anything to learn.

And yet …

And yet.

30.

VOICE

I was trying to find a voice. Trying to find my voice.
   Was I really a "writer?" No.

Was what I was doing "writing." No.

I was trying to save my soul.

I was in the paper bag of my own insanity and I was trying to write my way out.

Why was I trying to find a voice? I had no clue. If you had asked me, I couldn't even have articulated the idea that there was such a thing as "voice."

I was excruciatingly aware, however, not just that my writing was inauthentic, but that I myself was inauthentic.

Every word I wrote screamed of effort and fakery. I was self-conscious. I was full of shit. I didn't know what I was talking about.

Even when I was writing the absolute "truth," real events from my real life, the paragraphs came out hollow and phony.

I'd read Turgenev and Hemingway and Henry Miller. Every phrase rang like gold. Even the commas (or absent commas) were perfect. That was them talking. Why couldn't I do that?

I read Shakespeare, I read Marlowe, I read John Donne. Even when these writers weren't speaking as themselves, when they were writing in character, the voices sprang from a personality that was so profoundly entered into and so fully realized that it rang even truer than their own speech. The reading experience was hypnotic. It was healing. Even when I couldn't understand what these guys were saying, I felt my bones knitting just from the pace and rhythm of the work.

Why couldn't I do that?

Why was my stuff so bogus and so fake?

I used to sit down at the typewriter with *Tropic of Capricorn* or *The Sun Also Rises* open beside me. I would literally copy the books, word for word, paragraph by paragraph.

I was trying to experience a real voice, even if it wasn't my own.

31.

LETTERS

What helped, oddly enough, were my own letters. This was back in the days when people wrote letters. I'd write long ones to my friends. When I'd read them over, fixing typos, I'd stop sometimes and say, "Wow, that sounds like me."

How do we form ourselves?

By what means do we discover who we are?

The answer for us is the same as it is for characters in fiction. We discover who we are by what we say and what we do. We uncover our nature through action.

I began reading my letters over, slowly and carefully. What state of mind did I enter when I wrote to a friend? Was I "thinking?" Was I "trying?" Was I "writing?"

Maybe there's a clue there.

Maybe this is how you write.

32.

FINISHING

Beyond "voice," I was focused on one thing: Finishing.

Because I had crapped out 99.9 percent of the way through my first attempt at writing a novel (and because of the price in personal shame and the hurt my failure had inflicted on people I loved), I was obsessed with finishing Book #2 at all costs, come hell or high water, do it or hang myself.

I had to overcome my demons.

I had to face down my dragons.

An amateur, I knew, fades at the finish line.

A pro ... who was I kidding? I had no idea what a pro did.

33.

"REST IN PEACE, MOTHERFUCKER"

I wrote about this moment in *The War of Art*.

I worked for twenty-six months straight, taking only two out for a stint of migrant labor in Washington State, and finally one day I got to the last page and typed out:

> THE END.

I never did find a buyer for the book. Or the next one either. It was ten more years before I got the first check for something I had written and ten more after that before a novel, *The Legend of Bagger Vance*, was actually published. But that moment when I first hit the keys to spell out THE END was epochal. I remember rolling the last page out and adding it to the stack that was the finished manuscript.

Nobody knew what I had done. Nobody cared. But I knew. I felt like a dragon I'd been fighting all my life had just dropped dead at my feet and gasped out its last sulfuric breath.

Rest in peace, motherfucker.

Next morning, I went over to my writer friend Paul's for coffee and told him I had finished.

"Good for you," he said without looking up. "Start the next one today."

You must finish, over & over & over!

34.

GETTING OVER THE HUMP

If finishing was Obsession #1, getting over the hump was #2.

What do I mean by that? I couldn't have begun to articulate it at the time, but I felt it in every cell, waking and sleeping.

I knew I wasn't really writing. Not like real writers wrote. I was sitting in front of a typewriter and pounding out pages, even completing books, but what I was doing had nothing to do with real writing.

What *was* I doing?

I was using the act of writing (I should say the sham or simulacrum of writing) as a pretense to plant my own ego on the planet so that I could believe I really existed. Have you ever taken a selfie? That was it. That was what I was doing. It was like what people do today on Facebook and Instagram.

I was the hero of the books I was writing. I was the protagonist. I was the point of view. Everything happened to me.

I knew this was bullshit. I knew it was sick, it was sad, it was pathetic. I knew I had to get past it. I had to get over this hump or kill myself.

What was the hump?

One way to define it would be to say it was the watershed between the amateur and the professional. But that doesn't go deep enough.

A real writer (or artist or entrepreneur) has something to give. She has lived enough and suffered enough and thought deeply enough about her experience to be able to process it into something that is of value to others, even if only as entertainment.

A fake writer (or artist or entrepreneur) is just trying to draw attention to himself. The word "fake" may be too unkind. Let's say "young" or "evolving."

That was the hump.

To get over it, the candidate must grow up. A change has to happen at the cellular level.

I wrote one novel, and another, and another. Seven years full time, with gaps in between to earn money. And still I couldn't get over this hump.

A couple of years ago I re-read two of these first three manuscripts. I still have them. They're not terrible. But they are excruciating. Scanning a paragraph, I want to put myself up against a wall and slap the hell out of myself, and I would if I didn't have compassion for all of us who are compelled by the nature of life and the structure of the internal universe to go through this ordeal and initiation.

There seems to be no way to make the passage easier, nor any method to eliminate the pain. The lessons can't be taught. The agony cannot be inoculated against.

The process is about pain. The lessons come the hard way.

35.

MY FRIENDS

Ihad friends during these times. I had girlfriends. I wasn't alone in a bubble.

But it was clear to everyone I knew that I was riding the L train to nowhere, and it was clear to me that this was clear to everyone I knew. When I compelled my friends to read my stuff, the stiff, frozen nature of their smiles and the contortionist turns of phrase they were forced to employ to avoid telling me the truth were heartbreaking.

Poor Steve.

What will become of him? How will this end? Will we wind up fishing his body out of the Hudson? Which one of us will be IDing his corpse down at Bellevue? Will he become one of those drooling maniacs down on Canal Street? Will our wives recognize him behind a squeegee as he washes our windshield when we're in town going to a show?

This was all 100 percent clear to me.

Yet I couldn't stop writing.

Each time I left a job in advertising or any other field, my boss (who was always a friend as well) would call me into his office, close the door, and with the best of intentions give me The Speech.

He'd offer me a raise, a promotion. Steve, stay here on Planet Earth. Listen to reason. Don't flush your life down the toilet.

I knew my boss was right. My friend was flinging me a life preserver. What was wrong with me? Why wouldn't I take it?

Why couldn't I?

36.

AND YET ...

And yet you're learning. You don't know what. You can't say how. But the months and years, the millions of keystrokes and erasures go into the bank somehow. The cells remember. Something changes.

I was thirty-six, in New York City, when I finished the third of these multi-year books. Was there a glimmer? Please.

In the screenwriting trade, there's a concept called the All Is Lost moment. This moment usually comes about three-quarters of the way through the movie. It's the point in the story when the protagonist is farthest away from his or her goal.

In the celluloid world, the All Is Lost moment is always followed by a breakthrough, a turnaround beat when despair becomes hope (or desperation that's the equivalent of hope) that propels the protagonist into action in Act Three.

Here was mine:

Hollywood.

I thought, "I've been writing TV commercials for years. I know what film is. I can think visually. I love movies."

A screenplay.

I'll write a screenplay and move to Tinseltown.

BOOK THREE

HOLLYWOOD

37.

THREE-ACT STRUCTURE

In Los Angeles I starved for about five years. I wrote nine screenplays on spec. Each one took about six months. I couldn't sell any of them.

But I learned what a screenplay is.

I learned the principles of screenplay structure.

A movie script is composed of three acts. Act One: page 1 to about page 25. Act Two: page 25 to about page 75-85. Act Three: to the finish, page 105-120.

When someone first told me this (no doubt another fledgling writer) I immediately thought, "What formulaic bullshit! I'm not gonna be a slave to that!"

Wrong.

If there is a single principle that is indispensable to structuring any kind of narrative, it is this:

Break the piece into three parts—beginning, middle, and end.

Why is three-act structure essential in a movie?

Because a movie (or a play) is experienced by the audience in one continuous block of time. It's not like a novel or a piece of long-form nonfiction, which may be picked up and put down by the reader multiple times before she finishes. With a movie or a play, the audience enters the theater, settles in for ninety or 120 continuous minutes. You, the writer, have to keep them riveted in their seats for that length of time.

How do you do that?

By hooking them (Act One), building the tension and complications (Act Two), and paying it all off (Act Three).

That's how a joke is told. Setup, progression, punch line.

It's how any story is told.

Have you ever tried to seduce somebody? The hook, the build, the payoff.

Ever tried to sell somebody something?

Ever gotten in trouble and tried to talk your way out of it?

The hook, the build, the payoff.

Euripides worked in three acts. Shakespeare did.

Do you know something they don't?

38.

THE BOSS DEMONSTRATES THREE-ACT STRUCTURE

ACT ONE

I met her in a Kingstown bar.
We fell in love. I knew it had to end.

ACT TWO

We took what we had
and we ripped it apart.

ACT THREE

Now here I am, down in Kingstown again.

39.

FLASH FORWARD TO LONG-FORM FICTION: THE DAVID LEAN RULE

David Lean was the masterful film director of *Lawrence of Arabia*, *Doctor Zhivago*, *The Bridge on the River Kwai* and many others. He had a principle that applies beautifully not just to movies but to novels and to other long-form fiction and nonfiction.

Lean said, "Every work can be divided into between eight and twelve major sequences."

This is an alternative to the idea of Three-Act Structure.

Three-Act Structure works great in movies and plays, i.e., works that are experienced by the audience in one ninety- to 120-minute gulp.

But novels aren't like that. Long-form TV isn't like that. These forms are taken in by the reader or viewer at intervals, over periods of days, weeks, months. The rhythm of consumption is slower, with less need for pace or momentum.

In addition the reader or viewer tuning in to episode 12 needs a beat or two to bring back to mind everything that happened in episodes 1 to 11.

Watch *Lawrence of Arabia* carefully. You'll see that David Lean followed his own rule. The movie is constituted of focused, slowly-building, unhurried sequences, each of which may contain ten, fifteen, twenty scenes.

Each sequence is like a movie within a movie, and each sequence sets the stage for the sequences that follow.

Because of this, the story unspools with an epic grandeur. It feels stately, majestic, monumental.

40.

MOVIES ARE ABOUT GENRE

When my writing partner Stanley and I were searching for a new idea, the first question we'd ask ourselves was, "What kind of movie do *we* want to see?"

Do we wanna see a thriller?

A love story?

An apocalyptic superhero saga?

In other words, we were debating genre.

What genre would be fun to write in? What genre is hot right now at the box office? What genres should we definitely stay away from?

I love westerns and film noirs. Alas, both have been dead as genres for years.

Genre may be the most important single factor, from a writer's point of view, both in crafting the work and in attempting to find a market for it.

(For the definitive discussion on this subject, read Shawn Coyne's *The Story Grid*.)

Why is genre so important for the writer?

Because every film (and novel and play) falls into a genre, and every genre has its own ironclad, unbreakable rules.

41.

EVERY PIECE FALLS INTO A GENRE, AND EVERY GENRE HAS CONVENTIONS

Beating the hero up always works. *Cool Hand Luke*. *The Grapes of Wrath*. Every James Bond movie.

A Hero at the Mercy of the Villain scene plays because it's a convention of a genre.

If our Western has two gunslingers, they have to shoot it out in the final reel. If our Detective Story has a cop and a criminal, the rivals have to clash in the climax. If our Love Story features a pair of lovers, the two must move apart in the story's middle before they come together at the story's end.

That's not formula.

Those are genre conventions.

The writer must know what genre he is working in and the conventions of that genre, just as the bridge builder must understand the science of foundational integrity and the means of mitigating stress on strung steel.

Why?

Because a story (whether it's a movie, a play, a novel, or a piece of nonfiction) is experienced by the reader on the level of the soul. And the soul has a universal structure of narrative receptors.

Jung was right. There *is* a collective unconscious. Joseph Campbell was right. Myths and legends *do* constitute the fabric of the self.

The soul judges a story's truth by how closely it comports to the narrative templates that are part of our psyche from birth. The Hero's Journey. Odysseus. Gilgamesh. Buffalo Wallow Woman.

It's okay to blend genres (in fact, it's great if you can pull it off), but before we do that, we the writers must know the rules of the genre as well as a brain surgeon understands the topography of the cerebellum and the synaptic architecture of the neocortex.

42.

THE HERO'S JOURNEY

The first *Star Wars* came out about ten years before I started working in the movie industry. By that time, the concept of "the hero's journey" (upon which George Lucas had patterned Luke Skywalker's odyssey) had permeated Hollywood from top to bottom.

The mega-success of *Star Wars* had made every studio exec ask of any potential movie project, "Where is its 'hero's journey'? What scene represents 'the Call'? Which character is 'the Mentor'? Which 'allies and enemies' does the hero encounter along the way?"

What *is* the hero's journey anyway?

The hero's journey is the Ur-Story of every individual from Adam and Eve to Ziggy Stardust. It's the primal myth of the human race, the cosmic pattern that each of our lives (and a thousand increments thereof) follows, whether we know it or not, whether we like it or not.

Here's the nutshell version:

1) Hero starts in Ordinary World.
2) Hero receives Call to Adventure.
3) Hero rejects Call.
4) Hero meets Mentor. Mentor gives hero courage to accept Call.

(If you're following along, this is Luke on the evaporator farm. Luke finds R2D2, Luke uncorks distress hologram from Princess Leia, Luke takes R2 to Obi-Wan Kenobi.)

5) Hero crosses Threshold, enters Special World.

6) Hero encounters enemies and allies, undergoes ordeal that will serve as his Initiation.

7) Hero confronts Villain, acquires Treasure.

8) The Road Back. Hero escapes Special World, trying to "get home."

9) Villains pursue Hero. Hero must fight/escape again.

10) Hero returns home with Treasure, reintegrates into Ordinary World, but now as a changed person, thanks to his ordeal and experiences on his journey.

Cue up any movie from *Casablanca* to *The Martian*, including films with seemingly rulebook-defying structures like *Pulp Fiction* or Charlie Kaufman's *Adaptation*.

At the heart of each, in one form or another, you will find the hero's journey.

43.

THE HERO'S JOURNEY
IN THREE ACTS

Are you beginning to see the contours of what makes a story a story? Can you see the universal architecture that underlies virtually every tale from the Norse sagas to *South Park* and *Keeping Up with the Kardashians*?

Three-Act Structure + Hero's Journey = Story.

44.

THE HERO'S JOURNEY, DEEPER VERSION

Beyond its utility as a cheat sheet for writing hit movies, what exactly *is* the hero's journey?

Who invented it?

Where did it come from?

What is its purpose?

According to C.G. Jung, the hero's journey is a component of the collective unconscious. Joseph Campbell identified it in the myths and legends of virtually every culture on earth. Jung found it arising spontaneously in the dreams and neuroses of his psychiatric patients.

The hero's journey arose, both men speculated, from the accumulated experience of the human race over millions of years. The hero's journey is like an operating system (or software in an operating system) that each of us receives at birth, hard-wired into our psyches, to help us navigate our passage through life.

The hero's journey acts as a template or a user's manual. It tells us, "This is how things work, how life works. This is the road map to the way your own life will unfold."

(Required reading: Joseph Campbell's *The Hero with A Thousand Faces*, C.G. Jung's *Two Essays on Analytical Psychology* and *Symbols of Transformation*, and, for the real Movieland nitty-gritty, Christopher Vogler's *The Writer's Journey*.)

45.

WHY STORIES WORK
AND WHY THEY DON'T

Four chapters ago, I wrote that a story "is experienced by the reader on the level of the soul. And the soul has a universal structure of narrative receptors."

What I meant was that the hero's journey template is percolating inside all of our psyches 24/7 (whether we're aware of it or not) and that unconsciously we set every other story—every book we read, every movie we see—alongside it and ask ourselves, also unconsciously, "Does this tale ring true?"

The hero's journey is our touchstone.

When the book or movie we're reading or watching jibes with this Ur-Story, we say it "works."

We know it works not with our heads but with our guts.

The tale moves us. It satisfies us emotionally. We come to its end feeling like we've just had a meal of steak and potatoes.

When the story doesn't comport to the hero's journey template (even though, again, we may be completely unconscious of this or have never even heard of the hero's journey), we set the book down or walk out of the theater unsatisfied and vaguely pissed off.

"I dunno," we say. "The story seemed to be missing something. It didn't grab me. I was bored. It fell apart at the end."

46.

EVERY GENRE IS A VERSION OF THE HERO'S JOURNEY

Why do genres have conventions?

Why do the gunfighters have to shoot it out at the end of a Western? Why do the lovers have to break up before they can make up in a Love Story? Why can't we as storytellers "be creative" and simply violate these conventions?

Because each of these (and every other convention in every other genre) is a station in that genre's version of the hero's journey. And the human psyche takes in and evaluates every narrative it sees or hears according to how closely that narrative comports to the beats and structure of the hero's journey.

Be groundbreaking, be experimental if you want. But remember, the human psyche is deeply conservative and rigid as a rock.

Now—what exactly are the principles of storytelling?

47.

EVERY STORY HAS TO BE ABOUT SOMETHING

The principles of storytelling are sometimes so obvious that we can't see them.

Of course, you say, a story has to be about something. But I challenge you. Read a thousand screenplays penned by aspiring writers. Nine hundred and ninety-nine will be about nothing (and I don't mean in a good way like *Seinfeld,* which by the way was never about nothing.)

What does it mean, "to be *about something*?"

Hamlet is about something.

The Godfather is about something.

The Walking Dead is about something.

Beneath the car chases and the sex scenes and the special effects, a book or movie that works is undergirded by a *theme*.

A single idea holds the work together and makes it cohere.

Nothing in that book or movie is not on-theme.

48.

EVERY FIRST ACT MUST HAVE AN INCITING INCIDENT

I took Robert McKee's class. It was called Screenplay Structure then. The class was three days—half of Friday and all day Saturday and Sunday. It cost $199, I think. The class was full of other aspiring screenwriters as well as actors and actresses, studio execs and development guys and gals.

We were all desperate to find out what made a movie work.

McKee delivered.

About an hour into Friday evening's class, he introduced the concept of the Inciting Incident.

What was revolutionary for me was not so much that specific idea (though indeed it changed everything about the way I worked) as the mind-blowing thought that this stuff could actually *be taught*.

You could study.

You could learn.

You could get better.

The Inciting Incident is the event that makes the story start.

It may come anywhere between Minute One and Minute Twenty-Five. But it must happen somewhere within Act One.

It had never occurred to me that a story needed to start. I thought it started all by itself.

And I certainly had never realized that the writer had to consciously craft that specific moment when the story starts.

49.

HOW DOES A STORY START?

Pat Solitano (Bradley Cooper) is being released from a mental hospital in Baltimore. We see, from the first few minutes of film, that he's got serious psychiatric issues.

These issues coalesce around Bradley's obsession with getting back together with his wife Nikki, who has him under a restraining order and is scared to death of his nuttiness.

But Bradley has a plan. He's going to prove to Nikki that he has gotten his act together. He's sane now; he's a new man. He has put himself on a fitness regimen; he has lost weight. He has a motto of self-improvement: "Excelsior." He has dedicated himself to maintaining a "positive attitude." With that, he is certain he can find a "silver lining" and put his broken marriage back together.

These are the opening nine minutes of David O. Russell's *Silver Linings Playbook*.

All of it is great. Every piece of info is necessary for the story.

But so far it's only the Setup.

The story hasn't started yet.

The story starts about ten minutes into the movie, when Bradley's buddy Ronnie (John Ortiz) and Ronnie's wife Veronica (Julia Stiles) invite Bradley to their house for dinner and there introduce him to Veronica's sister Tiffany (Jennifer Lawrence) who also, by the way, has significant mental issues.

Bradley knows Jennifer slightly from the neighborhood. But she was married then, to a police officer named Tommy. Tommy has since died. Jennifer is now a widow, i.e., available.

Minute Ten:

Jennifer walks into the room and faces Bradley.

Bradley looks at Jennifer.

Jennifer sees the way Bradley is looking at her.

Jennifer looks back at Bradley the same way.

In the audience we know in this instant that Bradley's plan of reuniting with his wife Nikki has just flown out the window.

That's the Inciting Incident.

The story has now started.

In the audience, we have no idea *how* Bradley and Jennifer are going to get together (and in fact the obstacles keeping them apart seem overwhelming) but we know from the megawatt romantic chemistry between them that it is going to happen.

The story is rolling.

50.

EMBEDDED IN THE INCITING INCIDENT IS THE CLIMAX

How can you tell when you've got a good Inciting Incident? When the movie's climax is embedded within it.

Apollo Creed picks Rocky Balboa out of the book of fighters and says, "I'm gonna give this chump a shot at the title." That's the Inciting Incident of *Rocky I*. As soon as we hear it, we know that the climax of the movie will be Apollo and Rocky slugging it out for the heavyweight championship of the world.

In *Taken*, sex traffickers kidnap Liam Neeson's daughter. In the moment Liam manages to get on the phone with the kidnappers. He tells them to let her go or else. He is, we realize, a trained killer himself. "I have a very specific set of skills and I'm going to use them to hunt you down and kill you." The villains wish him "Good luck" and hang up.

Embedded in this Inciting Incident is the climax of *Taken*: Liam catches up to the bad guys and … well, you know what happens.

Anticipation of experiencing the climax is what pulls us, the audience, through the movie. We can't wait to see Linda Hamilton go toe to toe with the Terminator, or Clint Eastwood shoot it out with Gene Hackman, or Neo and Morpheus blast their way clear of the Matrix.

If your Climax is not embedded in your Inciting Incident, you don't have an Inciting Incident.

51.

THE SECOND ACT BELONGS TO THE VILLAIN

I learned this from my friend Randall Wallace (who wrote *Braveheart*), who learned it from Steve Cannell, the maestro of a million plotlines from *The Rockford Files* to *Baretta* to *21 Jump Street*.

Again, this is not formula. This is a principle of storytelling.

Once the Alien is aboard the *Nostromo*, once the Great White Shark has started cruising the waters off Amity, once the *War of the Worlds* Tripods have appeared in New Jersey, keep them front and center. The scarier the monster, the deeper the jeopardy, and the deeper the jeopardy, the more emotion will be produced in the hearts of the audience.

This works for abstract villains too, like the looming market crash in *Margin Call*. Once this monster has been introduced, the filmmakers go back to it again and again and every time they do, the story gets tauter and the audience gets sucked in deeper.

(Or if you believe that the real villain of *Margin Call* is the moral catastrophe implied in the impending group decision by the executives to tank the world economy in order to save themselves and their company [yes, I believe that too], then the filmmakers have answered that as well. Every second act scene reeks with this looming decision and the soul-calamity it implies.)

The villain in *Silver Linings Playbook* is internal. It's

Bradley's Cooper's obsession with getting back together with his wife Nikki.

By the end of Act One, Bradley has met Jennifer Lawrence. Clearly she loves him. Clearly the two of them are made for each other.

Will Bradley blow this potentially great thing with Jennifer because he's so obsessed with getting back together with his estranged wife?

> TIFFANY
> Tell me about this Nikki thing. This
> "Nikki Love." I wanna understand it.

The movie comes back to this Monster again and again through Act Two. No action hero was ever invested more with dread of a villain than Jennifer Lawrence is of this antagonist that exists only inside the skull of the troubled young man she's in love with. Her pain and jeopardy throughout Act Two keep us riveted and rooting for her.

Keep the villain up front throughout the Second Act.

52.

EVERY CHARACTER MUST REPRESENT SOMETHING GREATER THAN HIMSELF

I had been in L.A. for about six years. My eyes had been opened to the principles of storytelling. When I watched a movie now, I studied it. When I read a book, I put it under the microscope.

I pored over the classics. How did Billy Wilder produce such drama in *Double Indemnity*? Why did Shakespeare make the inciting incident of *Hamlet* the appearance of Hamlet's father's ghost?

I had become a student.

I'd sit in coffee shops with other Tinseltown acolytes, dissecting dialogue by Robert Towne or analyzing character concepts from David Webb Peoples and Julius and Philip Epstein.

What made characters like Jake Gittes or William Munny or Rick Blaine so indelible?

Answer (or at least partial answer): each stands for some quality, some aspect of the story's theme that transcends his narrow significance as an individual.

This principle can be taken further.

Every critical prop, artifact, or article of wardrobe—the '58 Plymouth Fury in *Christine*, Meg Ryan's hairstyles in *When Harry Met Sally*, Matthew McConaughey's shirt in *Mud*—can (and should) represent something significant to the theme and the story.

In the final scene of *Godfather I*, as the capos of the

Corleone crime family assemble in the office of the former-and-now-deceased godfather (Marlon Brando) to declare their allegiance to the new don, his son Michael (Al Pacino), and one of these captains slowly and deliberately swings the office door closed, shutting out forever Michael's wife Kay (Diane Keaton) who is looking on from the outer room, we in the audience get it.

We understand what the office represents, what the capos represent, what Michael represents, what Kay represents, and what the closing door represents.

It is no accident that all these elements have come together in this culminating image. Each one has been conceived and set up by the filmmakers, scene by scene and moment by moment throughout the movie, with this ultimate convergence in mind.

Nor is it random (since this is, after all, a motion picture) that all these components are visual and thus require no dialogue to deliver their meaning.

That's moviemaking.

That's storytelling.

53.

MOVIES ARE PICTURES

Blake Snyder (who tragically died in 2009 at age fifty-one) is one of my favorite writers about movies. If you haven't read *Save the Cat!* and *Save the Cat! Goes to the Movies*, get them right away.

One of Blake's principles is Keep It Primal. A great movie, he believes, should be so basic, so soul-grounded, that it could be understood by a caveman.

In other words, without language. Without dialogue.

Have you ever watched a movie with the sound off? The great ones stand up completely. *High Noon. Seven Samurai. Unforgiven.*

To say, "Keep it primal," is to say, "Tell the story in pictures."

Thinking in pictures forces you to keep the stakes of your story primordial. We *see* the Bad Barons humiliate the Honest Landsmen in *Braveheart.* Our eyes show us Meryl Streep leaving her husband Dustin Hoffman with their small boy Justin Henry in *Kramer vs. Kramer.* We see Matt Damon marooned on the red planet in *The Martian.*

Each of these setups evokes primal emotion. They suck us in. They make us root for a specific outcome. And though the dialogue is Oscar-worthy in all of these films, the scenes including the climax play almost as well MOS (without sound).

Movies are pictures.

54.

START AT THE END

Every trade has its tricks. Here's one you learn as a writer in Movieland:

Start at the end.

Begin with the climax, then work backward to the beginning.

Carrie.

The Great Gatsby.

Thelma and Louise.

The ending dictates the beginning.

I'm a huge fan of this back-to-front method. It works for anything—novels, plays, new-business pitches, music albums, choreography.

First figure out where you want to finish.

Then work backward to set up everything you need to get you there.

55.

FLASH FORWARD TO NARRATIVE NONFICTION: START AT THE END

In 2014, Sentinel/Penguin published my book *The Lion's Gate*, about the Arab-Israeli War of 1967. The book was nonfiction. Every person was real, every event actually happened. The nature of the material could not have been more different from that of fiction or of an imagination-based movie.

Yet I used the exact same principle:

Start at the end.

Not only did I start at the end in writing the book, I started at the end in writing the Book Proposal, i.e., the fifty-page document that would be submitted to publishers with the intention of making a deal so that I'd have the money to write the book.

It worked.

If you and I know the climax of *The Martian* (Mark Watney [Matt Damon] gets back safely to earth with a little help from his friends), our task in writing the book/movie becomes exponentially easier. We just have to come up with escalating obstacles that Mark/Matt (and his allies on Earth and in space) must overcome.

56.

FLASH FORWARD TO NARRATIVE NONFICTION: DO HOLLYWOOD RULES STILL APPLY?

Working out the structure for the nonfiction *The Lion's Gate*, I asked myself the same questions I would have asked had I been pitching the material to Twentieth-Century Fox.

What's the genre?

What's the theme?

What's the climax?

Who's the hero?

Who's the villain?

What are the stakes?

What is the jeopardy?

Exactly as with writing a screenplay, I started at the end and worked backward.

Are you a CEO preparing a speech for your stockholders? Write it like a novel or a movie. Use the principles of storytelling.

Write your Ph.D. dissertation the same way. And your grant proposal. And your plea to your landlord not to raise your rent.

Stories work.

Tell it to me as a story.

57.

STAKES

My first paying job in Hollywood was writing a script with the director Ernie Pintoff. We worked side by side at a big oak table in Ernie's kitchen.

Every time we got stuck, Ernie said the same thing:

"Have a body hit the floor."

He was talking about stakes.

Why do so many characters get killed (or threatened with being killed) in books and movies? Because it raises the stakes of the story to life and death.

How high should the stakes be in your story?

As high as possible.

High stakes = high emotional involvement by the audience.

That's why so many movies are about the end of the world. Invaders from space, pestilence, collision with an asteroid, Zombie Apocalypse.

They all work to raise the stakes.

A cheap trick, you say.

Yes. But it works.

Make the stakes life and death for your hero or for someone he/she loves. Or take it beyond life and death to damnation. Extinction of the soul. A fate worse than death. *The Pawnbroker. The Turn of the Screw. In the Valley of Elah.*

This stuff sounds like formula, I know. But it is the marrow and sinew of storytelling, and if you don't believe me, please check with Mr. W. Shakespeare.

58.

JEOPARDY

This is another Tinseltown trope that, dumb as it sounds, works.

Get your characters in danger as quickly as possible and keep ratcheting up that jeopardy throughout the story.

The more jeopardy to your characters, the more the audience will care and the more involved they will become.

Jeopardy doesn't have to mean bullets and bombs. In *Clueless* the peril is of being judged uncool. In *Ferris Bueller's Day Off* it's getting in trouble with Mom and Dad. But these perils are life and death in the worlds of Alicia Silverstone and Matthew Broderick.

Jeopardy and Stakes are twin sides of the same coin.

Our characters must, with life-and-death desperation, want or need some Thing or Outcome (stakes). Then their hold on, or hope for acquiring that Thing or Outcome must be thrust into grave-and-getting-graver peril (jeopardy).

Alan Alda, in an acting master class on HBO, had one of his students perform an exercise. He filled a glass to the brim with water and put it in the hands of the student. "If one drop spills," he told her, "every person in your hometown will die. Now, walk thirty feet across this stage and set the glass safely on top of that piano."

Trust me, not one soul in that audience drew a breath until the student had successfully navigated to the far shore. She herself looked like she was about to have a heart attack.

Stakes.

Jeopardy.

They work.

59.

TEXT AND SUBTEXT

There's an exercise that actors do in class:

A male student and a female student (or it could be same-sex) sit side by side on the stage. The teacher gives them a bland innocuous script, something about grocery shopping, say, or watching a cat play with a ball of yarn.

But the teacher instructs the students to play the scene as if they were seducing each other.

> JANE
> … yeah, the yarn kept unspooling across
> the carpet …

> JIM
> No kidding. What color was it?

The script is the text.

The seduction is the subtext.

The actors' challenge is to communicate via non-verbal means an unfolding narrative that is as far from the text as possible.

Have you seen the movie *True Confessions*? Robert De Niro and Robert Duvall play brothers in 1940s Los Angeles. Duvall is a much-compromised homicide detective, De Niro a powerful monsignor, a rising star in the L.A. archdiocese.

The brothers' relationship is strained throughout the

picture, with De Niro seemingly disapproving of Duvall's corruption-filled world—until a moment near the end of the film when, sitting side by side at a luncheonette counter, De Niro the monsignor confesses that his seemingly perfect inner world is in fact deeply, fatally troubled.

Duvall takes in this revelation, pauses for a long moment, then motions with one hand toward the dessert tray on the counter.

ROBERT DUVALL
Want something? Pie?

I'm sure I was not the only member of the audience who had to choke back a sob in that instant.

That's writing.

That's movie writing.

(And pretty good acting by Robert Duvall.)

The power of the performance comes from the contrast between the two levels of expression: what is being said (text) and what is being communicated by non-verbal means (subtext).

The greater the contrast, the more powerful the emotion produced in the audience.

The pleasure that we moviegoers derive from this juxtaposition of text and subtext comes from the fact that we get to participate in the moment. We watch and think, "See, Robert Duvall really loves his brother. Despite all the bad stuff between them, Duvall cares in the end."

The second half of the acting exercise from the start of this chapter takes place when the teacher halts the seduction scene and instructs the two students to use the identical bland script, only this time to play the scene as if one of them is about to murder the other, and the other one knows it.

> JANE
> … yeah, the yarn kept unspooling across
> the carpet.

> JIM
> No kidding. What color was it?

When I first got to Hollywood, I wrote scenes that were "on the nose." This is the most heinous crime a movie writer can commit. Dialogue that is "on the nose" expresses *exactly what is being portrayed non-verbally by the actors.*

> ROBERT DUVALL
> (puts arm around Robert De Niro)
> Brother, despite all our problems, I really
> care about you. Is there something I can
> do to help?

60.

DIGRESSION: HOLLYWOOD STORYTELLING

The story principles you learn in Hollywood share one primary quality:

They're very American.

Why are French films, or movies made in Japan or Iran or Israel. so different from homegrown U.S. pix? Because foreign stories arise from alien waters. The filmmakers don't share the same assumptions that we Yanks do.

1) American movies believe in the American Dream.

American stories start from the ground of freedom and equality. To us, these elements are universal. We take them for granted.

American stories buy into (and sell) the American dream—you can be anything you want to be if you're willing to work for it. And they deal with the American nightmare—what if we try and fail?

These are not universal verities or even universal aspirations.

The Taliban doesn't believe in them.

ISIS rejects them utterly.

American audiences love movies about long-shot successes—*Rocky* or *Rudy* or *Free Willy*. U.S. movies glorify outsiders and cranks. We love nerds and geeks and serial killers (if they're sympathetic) and vampires and werewolves and zombies. We love rebels, with a cause or without. We love mutants. The mutant is the supreme individual, supremely misunderstood. *X-Men, The Fan-*

tastic Four, even *Nebraska* and *The Big Bang Theory*. Be yourself, American movies say. Trust the Force.

Russian movies plumb far greater depths. America is adolescent; Russia is ancient. The Russian people have suffered famines and pestilence; they have endured defeat in war, violent revolution and more violent counter-revolution and all the personal and collective calamities that go with political and social upheavals on a monumental scale. *The Muppet Show* did not evolve in the U.S.S.R. There's no Russian Mickey Mouse.

Iranian movies go for individuality and idiosyncrasy to the point of universality. Israeli films are demanding and morally excruciating. Japanese flicks ascend to legend and timeless archetype.

2) American movies believe in cause and effect.

De Tocqueville called us Yanks a "race of mechanics." We invented the steam engine, the cotton gin, the flying machine. We understand gears and pulleys. We know how to use a socket wrench.

The American Dream is mechanical too. It believes in justice. If you and I work hard and play by the rules, success will be ours. This is an article of faith in the States (and is believed as fervently by each wave of immigrants flocking to U.S. shores.)

American movies reflect this optimistic belief. Just as you and I can fix our Ford V-8 if we faithfully apply the laws of mechanics, so too can we find the love of our life, bring the villain to justice, save the planet from apocalypse. We just have to *solve the problem*. As Tim Gunn says, "Make it work."

Does life *really* follow the laws of cause and effect? If you're asking that question, you're no doubt making movies in Budapest or Rangoon.

3) American movies are (with notable exceptions) irony-free.

Hollywood goes for the Big Finish. The lump in the throat, the orphan saved from the storm, the ninth-inning grand slam.

This is because our homegrown flicks believe in (and traffic in) the American Dream. So Harry finds Sally, Luke blows up the Death Star, Ripley whacks the Alien. In Walla Walla or the West Village, audiences would be furious if these movies ended any other way.

When you see an American movie with a tragic or ironic ending, the film has almost always been written or directed by a foreigner. Roman Polanski's *Chinatown*, Billy Wilder's *Double Indemnity*. Even *On the Waterfront* was made by Elia Kazan, who was Greek-American but way more Greek than American. And *Shane* is the exception that proves the rule.

So I'm not lobbying for the axioms in these chapters as timeless principles of storytelling that apply in all galaxies at all seasons of the year. These are Stars and Stripes principles. They grew out of, and so reflect, a very specific clime and place.

We must keep this in mind when we turn to the novel form and seek to move beyond three acts and beyond cause and effect.

61.

HOLLYWOOD STORYTELLING, PART TWO

Robert McKee articulates this commandment:
"Thou shalt not take the climax out of the hands of the protagonist."

What he means (and I agree completely) is, don't let your hero go passive in the movie's culminating crisis. Don't have some other character rescue him or her. Vin Diesel has to save the day in any movie with *Furious* in the title. James Bond must take down Spectre and no one else.

But this axiom, too, is thoroughly American.

It adheres to and celebrates the American Dream.

French movies frequently violate McKee's commandment, as do films from Scandinavia or Africa or Russia or Iran or Pakistan, or any Middle Eastern country.

Indian movies don't (at least the mainstream ones) but then the Indian Dream is more American even than the American Dream.

62.

WRITE FOR A STAR

Sometimes when we want to make our story "real," we scale back the dimensions of our characters. Makes sense, right? Real people are normal. Let's write a normal hero.

Wrong.

My first agent used to beat the hell out of me over this.

"Why are you writing a lead character like this? What actor is gonna want to play this schmuck? Can I give this to Kevin Costner? You're killing me!"

The audience wants to see a star.

Brad Pitt.

Angelina Jolie.

George Clooney.

Even Bruce Dern in *Nebraska* or Jack Nicholson in *About Schmidt*. These characters couldn't have been bigger losers. But they were stars.

What makes a role for a star?

1) His or her issues drive the story. Theirs and nobody else's. Every character in the story revolves around him or her.

2) His desire/issue/objective is (to him, in the context of his world) monumental. The stakes for him are life and death.

3) His passion for this desire/issue/objective is unquenchable. He will pursue it to, as Joe Biden might say, the gates of hell.

4) At the critical points in the story, his actions or needs (and nobody else's) dictate the way the story turns.

5) The story ends when his issues are resolved and no sooner.

Here are three roles played in the past few years by Matthew McConaughey: Ron Woodroof in *Dallas Buyers Club*, Mud in *Mud*, Rust Cohle in *True Detective*.

Each character's issues drive the story. Each character's passion is unquenchable. Each character is a star.

Put that kind of role at the center of your story and everything else will fall into place.

63.

WRITE FOR A STAR, PART TWO

The reason you have to write for a star in Hollywood is that a script is nothing until it's made into a movie. The medium is motion pictures, not screenplays.

And to make a motion picture (to get it funded, produced, distributed), you need a star.

What does that mean for you and me, the writers?

In the previous chapter, we've delineated a number of qualities that a star-worthy role requires. Here's another:

> The character must undergo a radical change from the start of the film to the finish. She has to have an arc. She must evolve.

Think of the roles Meryl Streep has played—Karen Blixen in *Out of Africa*, Karen Silkwood in *Silkwood*, Francesca in *The Bridges of Madison County*. It's no accident that each one of these characters undergoes a near-total transformation through the course of the movie. Ms. Streep would not have said yes to the role if they didn't.

But it starts with the writer. The writer wrote for a star. The writer created a role worthy of a star.

64.

BIG THEME = BIG STAR

How do we write for a star?

Not necessarily by concocting high-testosterone car chases or steam-up-the screen sex scenes.

We establish a theme *that is worthy of a star.*

Remember, the protagonist embodies the theme.

The more powerful the theme, the more powerful the starring role that will carry it.

Consider the character of Baroness Karen Blixen (Meryl Streep) in the movie *Out of Africa.*

The theme of *Out of Africa* is ownership.

Is it possible, the movie asks, for a human being to truly possess something—a lover, a farm, a dream?

Karen believes it *is* possible. In fact her whole life is founded upon this conviction. Her lover Denys Finch-Hatton (Robert Redford) teases her about this in one scene, chiding her gently for her habit of referring to "*my* school, *my* Kikuyu, *my* Limoges."

Karen also wants Denys to be "hers." She forbids him to go on safari with another woman and when he will not stand for this, she breaks off their romance.

In the end of course Karen loses everything—her farm, her dream of Africa, and Denys as well, who is killed tragically in a plane crash.

KAREN BLIXEN
Now take back the soul of Denys
Finch-Hatton. He brought us joy and we

> loved him well. He was not ours. He was
> not mine.

Life teaches Karen in the end that she cannot "own" anything. No one can. In defeat she sells her farm and sails home to Denmark, never to return to her beloved Africa.

But the brilliance of the conception of the film/theme/protagonist does not end here. For we in the audience know that the real-life Karen did in subsequent years reinvent herself as "Isak Dinesen" and go on to write a number of enduring works of fiction and nonfiction, foremost among them the book upon which the movie is primarily based, *Out of Africa*.

Not only is the film's theme one of profound depth and maturity, but this theme has been realized and rendered by the very person who suffered its agonies in real life.

Karen Blixen the woman may have been vanquished by the imponderables of life, at least in her dream of possessing something that would prove to be permanent. But Isak Dinesen the artist has triumphed, so much as that word may apply in such a tale, by producing a work of depth and beauty about that very tragedy.

Indeed Meryl Streep, the actress, brought her own star power to the role of Karen Blixen.

But the role, as brought forth by screenwriter Kurt Luedtke and director Sydney Pollack, already possessed superstar brilliance because of its placement at the epicenter of the movie's thematic architecture.

That's why Meryl Streep wanted to play it.

65.

A COROLLARY TO "WRITE FOR A STAR"

Don't be afraid to make your hero suffer.

Suffering is drama.

Actors love to suffer, and audiences love to watch them in torment.

The greater the ordeal we can put our protagonist through (*Cool Hand Luke, Philadelphia, The Revenant*), the more an actor or actress will want to play that part.

66.

WRITE FOR A STAR, PART THREE

Give the star an inner and an outer journey.

Car chases and passionate love affairs are great fun onscreen, but by themselves they will not attract a star.

A star wants an interior arc as well.

Why are James Bond movies, beloved and profitable as they may be, so lame? Because Mr. B. never changes. He has no interior journey. Can you blame Sean Connery (and now Daniel Craig) for seeking other, meatier roles? If 007 were all these performers were known for, they would never be taken seriously as actors.

Jack Nicholson, Meryl Streep, Tom Hanks, Julianne Moore, Jeff Bridges (we could name many others) will not touch a role, even a comic one, that doesn't have at least one (and preferably more than one) interior dimension.

67.

WRITE FOR A STAR, PART FOUR

The last and possibly most important quality that the writer must include in writing for a star is this:

A star wants to be unforgettable.

Actors, remember, are thinking in terms of their careers. They want to pile up roles that, over time, create a film persona that will endure.

Tom Hanks in *Splash, Big, Philadelphia, Saving Private Ryan, Forrest Gump, Apollo 13, Cast Away, Captain Phillips, Sleepless in Seattle, Bridge of Spies*. The characters Hanks plays in these films are not all "heroes." They don't all "win." They're not all "good."

But they all have scale. They possess depth. Their passages are star turns. They are one of a kind.

They are unforgettable.

Diane Keaton in *Annie Hall, Reds, The Godfather I* and *II, Manhattan, Interiors, Crimes of the Heart, Something's Gotta Give.*

Jack Nicholson in *Five Easy Pieces, Chinatown, Reds, One Flew Over the Cuckoo's Nest, Prizzi's Honor, Terms of Endearment, The Last Detail*, not to mention *The Shining, As Good as It Gets*, and *Easy Rider*.

It's an empowering exercise for us as writers to assess our protagonists by the criteria a star would apply when contemplating the role.

Would Jack Nicholson play this part? Bradley Cooper? Denzel Washington?

Could we attract Julia Roberts? Reese Witherspoon? Jennifer Lawrence?

Does our protagonist have a star arc? Have we given her star scenes? Does she suffer like a star? Evolve like a star?

Is she one of kind?

Is she unforgettable?

68.

FLASH FORWARD: WRITE FOR A STAR IN FICTION

Everything that is true for heroes in movies is true for protagonists in novels.

Indeed our book stands on its own—we don't have to cast an actor. But the hero or heroine of our work of fiction needs to possess the same scale and depth, the same star quality, star centrality, star arc and star suffering as if he or she were the lead in Hollywood movie.

Huck Finn.

Emma Bovary.

Captain Ahab.

Anna Karenina.

Hamlet.

Atticus Finch.

Holden Caulfield.

These are stars. And their passages and ordeals and triumphs are the stuff of starring roles.

Yeah, we can mock Hollywood and its predictable, formulaic conventions. But the old-time moguls (and even the contemporary bet-hedging, Twitter-driven, focus-group-dependent variety) knew something that we literary types sometimes forget.

The story's gotta play.

It's gotta put asses in the seats.

And nothing does that better than having, at the center of our tale, a huge star doing her huge star thing.

69.

THE ALL IS LOST MOMENT

Continuing on the subject of heroes, let's turn for a moment to our protagonist's darkest hour.

The All Is Lost Moment comes toward the end of Act Two in any movie. Look for it. Minute 72 to Minute 78. It'll be there.

And don't think that Jennifer Lawrence and Scarlett Johansson and Chris Pratt and Chris Hemsworth don't turn first to these exact pages when they read your script.

Why is the All Is Lost Moment so important?

Because the darker the hero or heroine's midnight hour, the more powerful will be their ultimate triumph/salvation/resolution—and the more emotional will be the audience's identification and involvement with him or her.

In the All Is Lost Moment, the Gal knows for sure that she's never gonna get the Guy; the Drunk is certain that he can never beat his dependence on alcohol; the Compassionate U.N. Dude knows he has no chance of holding back the Zombie Apocalypse.

Life is like that, isn't it?

That's why we in the audience can relate.

How many All Is Lost Moments have we ourselves had?

Your job as a writer is to give your hero the deepest, darkest, most hellacious All Is Lost Moment possible—and then find a way out for her.

70.

THE EPIPHANAL MOMENT

The All Is Lost Moment is followed almost immediately by a breakthrough insight or epiphany, an awakening for the hero, an "Aha!" moment.

From this point, the pedal-to-the-metal rush into Act Three and the story's climax begins. This epiphanal moment fuels and defines that rush.

Here's the epiphanal moment in the first *Rocky*:

ROCKY
... it's true, Adrian. I was nobody. But that don't matter either, you know? 'Cause I was thinkin', it really don't matter if I lose this fight. It really don't matter if this guy opens my head either. 'Cause all I wanna do is go the distance. Nobody's ever gone the distance with Creed, and if I can go that distance, you see, and that bell rings and I'm still standin', I'm gonna know for the first time in my life, see, that I weren't just another bum from the neighborhood.

This is one of the most satisfying and insightful epiphanies in movie history. Because:

1) It's totally organic; it comes out of Rocky alone, with no input from any external source.
2) It offers no magic bullet to Rocky's predica-

ment. Instead it indicates that he, our hero, recognizes that no conventional positive resolution is possible within his dilemma.

The issue from the All Is Lost Moment ("Who am I kiddin'? I can never beat the champ. He's gonna wipe the floor with me") is not resolved by this epiphany. The fight remains. Rocky still has to get into the ring and fight the champ.

3) It delivers a truth that the hero has been in denial of. The hero faces this truth squarely. He ceases to be in denial of it.

4) That truth is painful, and at first it seems to set the hero back. But it is also tremendously empowering because the hero is now standing on solid ground. When he accepts that and moves forward, he is acting from truth.

The All Is Lost moment in *Fury* comes when S/Sgt Don "Wardaddy" Collier (Brad Pitt) and his tank crew including Boyd "Bible" Swan (Shia LaBeouf) have their tank disabled by a mine just as a battalion of German SS troops is spotted marching down the road straight at them. The Yanks decide to stand and fight, even though they know it will mean their deaths. Inside the tank, moments away from this fatal confrontation, the crew passes around a bottle of whisky.

BRAD PITT
(toasts to tank and crew)
Best job I ever had.

The crew laughs darkly. This catch-phrase is something we in the audience have heard the crew say to one another, with grim humor, in prior dire moments in the film. Pitt now passes the bottle to LaBeouf.

> SHIA LEBEOUF
> Best job I ever had.

This epiphanal moment fulfills all four points cited above.

From the epiphanal moment in *Rocky,* the audience is asking only one question: "Will Rocky be able to go the distance with the heavyweight champ, Apollo Creed?"

From this epiphanal moment in *Fury,* we in the audience are wondering only one thing: "How are these guys gonna die and what damage will they do before that?"

A great epiphanal moment not only defines the stakes and the jeopardy for the protagonist and for the audience, but it restates the theme and answers the question, "What is this story about?"

71.

GIVE YOUR VILLAIN
A BRILLIANT SPEECH

The point is, ladies and gentlemen, that greed, for lack of a better word, is good. Greed is right, greed works. Greed clarifies, cuts through, and captures the essence of the evolutionary spirit. Greed, in all its forms: greed for life, for money, for love, knowledge has marked the upward surge of mankind. And greed, you mark my words, will not only save Teldar Paper, but that other malfunctioning corporation called the U.S.A.

Michael Douglas/Gordon Gekko's "Greed is good" speech from *Wall Street* may be the greatest movie villain speech ever. Hats off to Stanley Weiser and Oliver Stone who wrote it.

A classic Villain Speech must accomplish at least two objects:

1) It must allow the antagonist to state his or her point of view as clearly and powerfully as possible.

2) It must be so rationally stated and so compelling in its logic that we in the audience (or at least a part of us) find ourselves thinking, "Hmm, this villain is evil as hell—but we have to admit, he/she's got a good point."

Why is a brilliant Villain Speech so important?

Because the greater and more interesting the villain, the greater and more interesting the hero—and the more satisfying his or her triumph over the foe.

When Satan tempted Jesus in the wilderness, what argument did he make? What was the exact text of his speech?

I don't know, but I would've loved to have heard it. Wouldn't you?

72.

KEEP THE VILLAIN HUMAN

Remember, the antagonist carries the counter-theme. The more clearly and powerfully we the writers can articulate this in a Villain Speech (or by some other, purely visual or non-verbal means), the more deeply the audience will be drawn into the story and the more powerfully their emotions will be engaged.

JAKE GITTES
How much are you worth? Ten million?

NOAH CROSS
Oh my, yes!

JAKE GITTES
Why are you doing it? What could you buy that you can't already afford?

NOAH CROSS
The future, Mr. Gittes! The future. Now, where's the girl? I want the only daughter I've got left. As you found out, Evelyn was lost to me a long time ago.

JAKE GITTES
Who do you blame for that? Her?

NOAH CROSS
I don't blame myself. You see, Mr. Gittes,
most people never have to face the fact
that at the right time and the right place,
they're capable of ANYTHING.

If the value at stake in a detective story is justice, and
the detective/hero (Jack Nicholson in Robert Towne's
classic scene from *Chinatown* above) represents the search
for that commodity, then the villain (John Huston) must
represent its opposite.

But to make the villain a pure monster is a cheat. He
must be recognizably and relatably human. If our story is
to achieve its maximum power, we the writers must deliver to the audience the blood-freezing realization that a
part of them, too, believes that greed is good, and that
they too, under a certain set of circumstances, would be
capable of performing the unspeakable.

73.

HOW WE LEARN

You don't really learn an art or a craft in school. In the real world, the process is more like an apprenticeship, multiple apprenticeships under multiple masters. It happens on the street and it happens in the studio. It happens in bed. It happens sober and it happens stoned. It happens getting up early and it happens staying up late.

You move to L.A., New York, London.

You make friends.

You form relationships at your own level, the novice class. And you make friends at the mentor level, above you. You kiss ass. You work for free. You do stuff that nobody else will do.

You work on your own and you team up with others. You save your pennies. You decide you'll do a web series or shoot your own film or write a screenplay on spec. Day One, your buddy says, "What's our Break Into Two?"

"Break Into Two? What the hell's that?"

That's how you learn.

You take a class. You sign up for a webinar. Maybe you literally go back to school and get a degree. You read a million scripts and a million books about scripts. You submit material and people critique it.

In other words, you're in the trenches, getting hosed and head-banged and dismissed and ignored. You're invisible. You're held in contempt. You're exploited.

People farther up the food chain take your time,

your energy, your body. You let them. You want them to take these things. It's the price you pay to learn.

I love shows like *Project Runway* or *Top Chef*. You don't even have to have the sound on. "Make it work," says Tim Gunn.

That's how you learn.

You start out with friends who are as broke as you and as clueless. Then one gets hired somewhere. It's the same in the music biz or the rag trade or dance or photography or video game design. That one friend pulls the others up. She calls you in for a free rewrite. "Can you deliver overnight?" Of course you can.

That's how you learn.

You take jobs because you're broke that you would never take if you had any pride or self-respect or cash. I did a rewrite once on an all-time sleazeball porn flick. I lost a girlfriend over it.

But I learned more in four days than in a semester at the Yale Drama School.

Then there's the way you *really* learn:

Alone at your keyboard.

Alone in the dance studio.

Alone in the darkroom.

Trying to answer the Eternal Question: "Why is this fucking thing not working?"

Creative work can be hell, but it can be heaven too. What could be better than beating your brains out on a problem that's *exactly the problem you need to solve to get better?*

We learn by increments. One word, one image, one piece of code at a time. A screenwriter may have fifty scripts in her closet. She can take you to a line in #3 or #17 or a scene in #31 or all of Act Two in #47 and tell you how it took her all day or all week or all month to solve that particular problem.

That's how you learn.

A perennial query: Should I move to Los Angeles if I want to write for the movies or TV? Do I have to pack up for New York if I want to work in fashion? My dream is to be in adult films; do I have to move to the San Fernando Valley?

You do.

That's how you learn.

74.

SAYONARA, TINSELTOWN

I worked for another five years as a solo screenwriter. I got better. I was writing much smarter stuff than I did with Stanley, and it felt better that it was all mine. I could do it. I felt like a pro. I was a pro.

Then I had the idea for *The Legend of Bagger Vance*.

The story came to me full-blown. I could see it, start to finish.

There was only one problem. The idea came *as a book,* not a movie.

The short version is I told my agent and he fired me. He told me he couldn't afford to wait for me while I went off to indulge my literary fantasies.

I made another decision.

Fuck my agent.

I'm gonna write the book.

BOOK FOUR

FICTION: THE SECOND TIME

75.

HOW CAREERS HAPPEN

My friend David Leddick says you can never plan your life because too many imponderables come into play. "You meet someone and you wind up living in another country, speaking a different language."

And yet …

And yet the arc of a career is not entirely random or shaped in the end by factors beyond our comprehension or control. I have felt my whole life that I've been on a course and being guided, even though I didn't know by what.

I started *Bagger Vance* with immense trepidation. Would I fall apart again, as I had every other time I'd tried to write something beyond 120 pages? What was different this time? Had I learned anything?

To my amazement, the tale poured out of me. Of course I was certain that no one would be interested in it. A golf story? With mystical dimensions? Please.

But I didn't care.

I was possessed.

When I looked up four years later, I had finished and published at the highest professional level three consecutive successes—*Bagger Vance, Gates of Fire*, and *Tides of War*, a 120,000-worder, narrating all twenty-seven years of the Peloponnesian War.

WTF?

What happened?

76.

MY OVERNIGHT SUCCESS

I'm fifty-one years old and my first novel is being published.

It was easy.

Why?

Because in writing that work, I was bringing to the field of fiction all the principles I had learned in twenty-seven years of working as a writer in other fields, i.e., writing ads, writing movies, writing unpublishable fiction.

1) Every work must be about something. It must have a theme.
2) Every work must have a concept, that is, a unique twist or slant or framing device.
3) Every work must start with an Inciting Incident.
4) Every work must be divided into three acts (or seven or eight or nine David Lean sequences).
5) Every character must represent something greater than himself/herself.
6) The protagonist embodies the theme.
7) The antagonist personifies the counter-theme.
8) The protagonist and antagonist clash in the climax around the issue of the theme.
9) The climax resolves the clash between the theme and the counter-theme.

I had learned these storytelling skills.

But other capacities that I had also acquired over the preceding twenty-seven years were even more important.

These were the skills necessary to conduct oneself as a professional—the inner capacities for managing your emotions, your expectations (of yourself and of the world), and your time.

1) How to start a project.
2) How to keep going through the horrible middle.
3) How to finish.
4) How to handle rejection.
5) How to handle success.
6) How to receive editorial notes.
7) How to fail and keep going.
8) How to fail again and keep going.
9) How to self-motivate, self-validate, self-reinforce.
10) How to believe in yourself when no one else on the planet shares that belief.

So … what have we learned about writing fiction the second time around?

77.

FICTION IS TRUTH

I never wrote anything good until I stopped trying to write the truth. I never had any real fun either.

Truth is not the truth.

Fiction is the truth.

The conventional truism is "Write what you know." But something mysterious and wonderful happens when we write what we *don't* know. The Muse enters the arena. Stuff comes out of us from a very deep source.

Where is it coming from? The "unconscious"? The "field of potentiality"?

I don't know.

But I've had the same experience over and over. When I write something that really happened, people read it and say, "Sounds like bullshit."

When I pull something completely out of thin air, I hear, "Wow, that was so real!"

78.

FLASH FORWARD: NONFICTION IS FICTION

When you work with fact, treat it as fiction.

Write your nonfiction book as if it were a novel. I don't mean make stuff up. That's a no-no. I mean give it an Act One, an Act Two, an Act Three. Make it cohere around a theme.

Give it a hero, and make that hero embody the theme.

Give it a villain, and make that villain stand for the counter-theme.

Make the narrative build to a climax, and have that climax resolve the conflict of the narrative in terms of the theme.

As I'm writing this book you're reading now, which has no story and no characters, I'm constructing it as if it were fiction, according to the conventions of a novel.

79.

NARRATIVE DEVICE

We're in Monroeville, Alabama, you and I, watching Harper Lee alone at her typewriter as she sits down to start *To Kill a Mockingbird*. How, Ms. Lee asks herself, do I tell this story?

"Do I tell it in the third person, as the Omniscient Author? Or should I have Atticus narrate it in the first person? Would it work if Tom Robinson told the story? Bob Ewell? Boo Radley?

"OMG ... Scout!"

Philip Roth's breakthrough in *Portnoy's Complaint* was to have Portnoy tell the story—and to do in one book-length monologue as if he were in a session with his shrink.

Johnny Depp found the voice for Capt. Jack Sparrow when he decided to play the part as if he were Keith Richards.

Narrative device asks four questions:

1) Who tells the story? Through whose eyes (or from what point of view) do we see the characters and the action?

2) How does he/she tell it? In real time? In memory? In a series of letters? As a voice from beyond the grave?

3) What tone does the narrator employ? Loopy like Mark Watney in *The Martian*? Wry and knowing like Binx Bolling in *The Moviegoer*? Elegiac like Karen Blixen/Isak Dinesen in *Out of Africa*?

4) To whom is the story told? Directly to us, the readers? To another character? Should our serial killer address himself to the detective who has just arrested him? To his sainted mother who believes he's innocent? To the judge who's about to sentence him to the electric chair?

These questions are make-or-break. If we get our narrative device right, the story will tell itself.

Here's one principle that has helped me:

Narrative device must work *on-theme*.

To Kill a Mockingbird is a story of decency and honorable action taken in the face of daunting, even terrifying adversity. Its hero, Atticus Finch, embodies an ideal of American manhood, like Daniel Boone or Abe Lincoln or any character played in the movies by Gary Cooper or Jimmy Stewart, in that he bears no pedigree; arrives on-scene supported by no escort or entourage; undergoes his ordeal of honor in an arena far from the sight of the multitude and proves his valor before only a modest number and, of those, is appreciated or even understood by very, very few.

Scout is perfect as the narrative device because we, the readers, are meant to see Atticus through the eyes of the daughter who worships him. And this daughter is not Scout *in the moment*, not Scout as the six- to nine-year-old she is during the events of the book, but Scout as a grown woman, seasoned by her own sorrow, recalling and reflecting upon the story from a remove of miles and years.

The narrative device embodies the theme.

Virtually by itself, it produces success for *To Kill a Mockingbird*, as it does for *Crime and Punishment* or *The Sun Also Rises* or *The Iliad*.

80.

NOVELS ARE ABOUT THE LONG GAME

A novel will take you two years to write. Or three or four or five.

Can you do that?

Can you sustain yourself financially? Emotionally? Can your spouse and children handle it?

Can you maintain your motivation over that length of time? Your self-belief? Your sanity?

If necessary, can you scrap your first eighteen months' work and start over from scratch?

81.

NOVELS ARE ABOUT IMMERSION

Writing a novel is an adventure. It really is.

I take my hat off to anyone who embarks on this journey and sees it through to completion because it's a life-changer. You can't write 290 pages, or 380, or 976 and not have it alter you.

A novel is too long to be organized efficiently like a screenplay. There aren't enough 3X5 cards in the world.

Too much shit happens.

New characters appear. New ideas show up. The whole story can get hijacked by the apparition of Mr. Micawber or Hamlet's ghost or Winnie the Pooh.

A novel is like an acid trip. For the first forty-five minutes you're thinking, "Hmm, this isn't so intense. I can handle this." Then you look down at your hands and flames are coming out of them.

82.

NOVELS ARE DANGEROUS

Writing a novel is not for the faint of heart.

Consider what you're letting yourself in for: a two- to three-year siege with no external validation or reinforcement, no paycheck, and no day-to-day structure except that which you impose yourself.

Support from friends and family? Dubious. Future rewards? Iffy at best. And we're not even talking about the work.

Will your significant other understand? The best advice for the mate of a novelist is to sit down, pour yourself a stiff brandy, and make sure in your heart that this is a starship you're really ready to blast off in.

No one, trust me, can write a novel and not become completely submerged in it. You have to or you can't keep going.

Think about how crazy that is.

You, the writer, are having conversations all day (and all night) with personalities who don't exist. Those with whom you spend every working hour, and about whom you care most passionately possess no corporeal reality. You're like Walter Pidgeon dueling the Monsters from the Id in *Forbidden Planet* (Netflix it if you haven't seen it).

You have entered a realm whose depths and dimensions are known to you alone. You can try to involve your spouse, yeah, but that glassy, semi-panicky look in his/her eyes is real. He/she has just realized that they're linked for life with a person they do not know.

One of the weirdest things in the world is to look in the mirror (I mean *really* look) when you're in the throes of writing a novel.

You don't even recognize yourself.

You are dealing with the Muse now. You are on her turf. She owns you.

You have ceded your psychic autonomy to forces based in a different dimension of reality. This is the Foreign Legion, baby, and I don't mean France.

It's a rush. It's *the* rush. But it also can scare the shit out of you.

I'm not kidding when I say that your closest, and possibly only confidant has now become your cat, your dog, your goldfish. They don't get you either, but at least they're not the mother or father of your children.

Why do so many novelists become drunks or addicts? Why do so many take the gas pipe?

You're playing with dynamite when you type

CHAPTER ONE.

83.

DUELING THE MONSTER

How do we handle the length of time and the degree of dedication that are required to complete any long-term, multi-year project?

The following chapters detail principles that have worked for me.

84.

THINK IN BLOCKS OF TIME

Writing a novel is like crossing the continent in a prairie schooner.

You, the pioneer, must master the art of delayed gratification. You have to break the trek down in your mind into mini-treks whose distance and demands your sanity can handle.

Can you do a first draft in three months?

Too daunting? How about a rough sketch in three weeks?

Still too scary? Maybe a rough-rough in seven days?

Remember, the enemy in an endurance enterprise is not time.

The enemy is Resistance.

Resistance will use time against you. It will try to overawe you with the magnitude of the task and the mass of days, weeks, and months necessary to complete it.

But when we think in blocks of time, we acquire patience. We break down that overwhelming transcontinental trek into doable daily or weekly transits. Drive our Conestoga wagon two thousand miles from Independence, Missouri to Oregon City, Oregon? No way!

But we can make it to Topeka in ten days and from there to Fort Riley in another twelve.

85.

THINK IN MULTIPLE DRAFTS

I'll do between ten and fifteen drafts of every book I write. Most writers do.

This is a positive, not a negative.

If I screw up Draft #1, I'll attack it again in Draft #2. I'll invoke the Jack "Top Gun" Epps rule:

You can't fix everything in one draft.

Thinking in multiple drafts takes the pressure off. We're not trying to build Rome in one day.

Thinking in multiple drafts is a corollary of thinking in blocks of time. If we know we're going to do fifteen drafts before we're done, we don't panic when Draft #6 is still a mess.

"Relax, we've got nine more tries to make it work."

The great thing about writing (as opposed to climbing Mt. Everest or raising children or going to war) is the work sits still.

What we did yesterday stays intact on the page, where we can rethink it, revise it, rework it tomorrow.

86.

SURRENDER TO THE MATERIAL

A screenplay, as we said, can be controlled. We can block out the structure. We can scrawl sixty scenes on 3X5 cards and pin them to the wall. We can contain the whole thing in our mind. We can see it in one piece.

But a novel is too big for that. Multi-season TV, like *Homeland* or *The Walking Dead*, is too big for that.

Big fiction has too many characters, too many twists and turns, too many serendipitous discoveries along the way.

You have to surrender to the material.

You have to put yourself at the service of the idea.

If there is a joy to writing (and there is), this is it for me.

When I was twenty-nine, as I said earlier, I moved from New York to Carmel Valley, California with enough money (saved from working in advertising) to rent a little house and dedicate a year to finishing a novel. No TV, no music, no sex. I did nothing but write all day and read all night.

There were two living beings in that house—me and the material.

It was a closed cage match to the death.

But at the same time it was a love affair.

You could fight the material, you could curse it, you could kick it with your knees or gnaw at it with your teeth, but sooner or later you had no choice but to surrender to it.

As artists, you and I are struggling each day to dominate our material, to shape it into a cohesive whole with a beginning, a middle, and an end. But at the same time, the raw entity defies us. It's a living thing, with its own power and its own destiny. It "wants" to be something.

Our job is to discover what that something is—and to help it become that.

87.

MASTER THE MATERIAL

When you surrender to the saga of Queen Boudica of early Britain, you immerse yourself in the historical material with the aim of finding that story, that version of the underlying truth that resonates with your own quirky, personal, idiosyncratic soul. Is it a love story? A redemption tale? A shield-banging, tub-thumping patriotic anthem?

But once you've found that story, you have to defeat it. How?

By enlisting the principles of storytelling and the conventions of the genre. You have to tame your story and domesticate it. You have to render it fit for human consumption.

Writerly self-indulgence ends here.

Now we must serve the reader.

88.

WHAT THE SCREENWRITER TAUGHT THE NOVELIST

The novelist has many tools and tricks that the screenwriter doesn't.

The novelist can write an entire book composed of nothing but love letters. She can write a book that's all recipes.

She can digress. She can go off on tangents. The rigid, momentum-driven imperative of the ninety-minute film doesn't apply to her. She's got time. Exposition? Backstory? She can simply tell it to us, in her own voice or the voice of one of her characters. She can take us inside her characters' heads. (All these are things the screenwriter can't do.) She can tell us what her characters are thinking, or have them show us or tell us themselves.

And she can use her mastery of language. She can bewitch us with the brilliance of her prose. She can seduce us with the charm of her voice or her narrator's voice. She is not shackled, like the movie writer, by being able to indicate character, and even narrative, only from the outside.

These are the advantages that the novelist possesses.

But her Tinseltown colleague, the screen or TV writer, has learned one trick that she, the novelist, may not know.

He has learned how to use structure.

William Goldman in *Adventures in the Screen Trade* famously declared that

Screenplays are structure.

He was right.

What makes the final scene of *The Martian* work (or the season-ending episode of *Downton Abbey* or the scene where the kitten finds Orson Welles in the doorway in *The Third Man*) is structure.

What came before sets up what follows. The moment pays off in Scene 57 because of what the writer laid in in Scene 4, Scene 19, and Scene 41.

This, the screenwriter can control.

The novelist can command this too.

Sometimes writers who begin their careers working in literary fiction or narrative nonfiction come to rely so heavily on their own command of language and other skills of the words-on-paper trade that they fail to fully exploit the power of structure.

Screenwriters think in structure because it's one of the few tools they have.

Screenwriters start at the end. They solve the story's climax first. Then they work backward. They layer in all the foundational material that the climax needs to deliver its emotional and thematic wallop.

This is a powerful skill to have when you move from starting your stuff with

FADE IN

and instead begin with

CHAPTER ONE.

89.

FLASHBACK: A NOVEL HAS TO HAVE A CONCEPT

Let's go back for a moment to our days in the ad game. An advertising campaign, we learned then, must have a concept.

How does that apply to fiction? What does it mean?

It means that we can't tell our great-great-grandmother's life story just because she crossed Oklahoma in a covered wagon and nearly got scalped by the Comanches.

We can't simply narrate an account of our two tours in Afghanistan.

Why not?

Because *nobody wants to read your sh*t*.

We cannot give our readers ore. We must give them gold.

Herman Melville went to sea a-whaling. Ernest Hemingway drove an ambulance in World War I. But the concept of *Moby Dick* is not "Lemme tell you what happened when I went a-whaling." And the concept of *The Sun Also Rises* is not "We had a rough time in the war."

Remember, a concept is a spin or a twist, a unique and original framing of material.

The concept of *The Big Lebowski* is "Let's take the genre of the Private Eye Story but make our hero not a hard-bitten detective but a sweet, loveable stoner."

The concept of *Huckleberry Finn* is "Let's satirize the fierce, brutish, small-minded racism of the pre-Civil War South by telling the story of the true friendship between a white boy and a runaway slave through the ironic (though he doesn't know it) cracker vernacular of the boy."

A great concept gives every word and every scene an interesting, illuminating spin. It takes ordinary and much-used material and makes it fresh.

The concept of *The Sun Also Rises* is "Let's describe the devastation wreaked by WWI on an entire generation, not by telling a war story but by telling a post-war story."

Does your novel have a concept?

Mad Men has a concept. *House of Cards* has a concept. *Breaking Bad* has a concept.

So do *Don Quixote, The Corrections,* and *Infinite Jest.*

Does your novel have a concept?

90.

FLASHBACK: A NOVEL HAS TO BE ABOUT SOMETHING

We're applying principles now that we learned in advertising and in Hollywood.

We're talking about *theme*.

Theme is *what the story is about*.

Theme is not the same as concept.

A concept is external. It frames the material and makes us look at every element of that material from a specific point of view.

A theme is internal. When we strip away all elements of plot, character and dialogue, what remains is theme.

The concept of *The Sopranos* is "Let's take a gangster and send him to a shrink. When he whacks somebody, he feels guilty about it. We'll show a crime boss suffering internally."

That's a terrific concept. Other than *Analyze This,* which treated this idea differently, it had never been done before.

That's the concept of *The Sopranos*.

The theme is "All of us are crazy in the same way. A gangster's inner turmoil is exactly the same as that of every other affluent suburbanite with a family and a job. The only difference is our protagonist regularly kills people."

It's possible for you and me to write a 1,000-page novel and have no idea what its theme is. I've done it more than once.

But if we can't articulate it, we have to have an iron-clad unconscious instinct for what it is.

From the first day I start to think about an idea for a novel, I ask myself, "What is this damn thing *about*?"

When I can answer that, I've got to key to every scene and every chapter.

91.

FLASHBACK: A NOVEL HAS TO HAVE A HERO

Sometime in the 1990s I was reading Herodotus' *The Histories* (for fun) when I came upon this passage:

> Although extraordinary valor was displayed by the entire corps of Spartans and Thespians, yet bravest of all was declared the Spartan Dienekes. It is said that on the eve of battle, he was told by a native of Trachis that the Persian archers were so numerous that, when they fired their volleys, the mass of arrows blocked out the sun. Dienekes however, quite undaunted by this prospect, remarked with a laugh, "Good. Then we'll have our battle in the shade."

That was the genesis of *Gates of Fire*. I knew instantly that I had found my hero and that, from him and this brief passage, would flow concept, theme, point of view, narrative device, villain, three-act structure, and crisis/climax/resolution.

I had only to do what I had learned working in the movies.

Write for a star.

92.

WRITE FOR A STAR IN FICTION

If we're making a movie we can cheat and simply cast a star.

We can't do that in a novel.

We have to *create* the star.

But how?

Consider Huck Finn.

Huck is a star role by any definition. But what makes him so?

Answer—the theme and concept of the overall work.

To make the protagonist a star, make the theme and concept a star.

Mark Twain's concept for *The Adventures of Huckleberry Finn* was to attack the issue of racism by telling the story of a friendship between a redneck Missouri boy and a runaway slave through the eyes of the boy himself—an unlettered but decent and great-hearted lad whose cracker culture had conditioned him to be reflexively and unbendingly racist.

Is that a brilliant concept or what?

As Huck and Jim become closer through their various shared adventures and Huck comes to understand in his heart what a true-blue friend Jim is and how brave and honorable and noble, Huck feels guiltier and guiltier.

His American South 1840-ish upbringing, which he sees as "proper" and "good," has instructed him, upon pain of eternal damnation, that he must not befriend Jim, not protect him, and certainly not help him escape to freedom.

In the story's moral climax, Huck takes into his hands the note he has just written to Miss Watson, which would turn Jim in as a runaway:

> It was a close place. I took [the letter] up, and held it in my hand. I was a-trembling, because I'd got to decide, forever, betwixt two things, and I knowed it. I studied a minute, sort of holding my breath, and then says to myself:
> "All right, then, I'll go to hell"—and tore it up.

In other words, the star power of the role of Huck Finn comes from the scale and moral weight of the book's concept and theme.

Huck is the protagonist. He embodies the theme. He is the personification of the theme.

Because the theme is profound and powerful and the concept brilliant and effective, Huck as their human vehicle is jam-packed with emotion and power and moral authority.

He's a star.

In other words, the power of the protagonist derives directly from the power of the theme and the concept.

Who cares if we as novelists don't have the luxury of casting George Clooney or Cate Blanchett?

We can create a starring role by writing it.

Write *Moby Dick* and we'll have Ahab.

Write *Crime and Punishment* and we'll have Raskolnikov.

Write *The Catcher in the Rye* and we'll have Holden Caulfield.

BOOK FIVE

NONFICTION

93.

NONFICTION IS FICTION, PART TWO

The first nonfiction work I wrote was *The War of Art*. The first narrative nonfiction was *The Lion's Gate*.

Neither one had characters that could be manipulated like those in fiction. Neither possessed an obvious narrative, nor a hero or villain, an Inciting Incident, an All Is Lost moment, a three-act structure, nor an immediately apparent crisis/climax/resolution.

Yet I wrote both of them as if they did, and it worked.

That's what I mean by nonfiction is fiction.

If you want your factual history or memoir, your grant proposal or dissertation or TED talk to be powerful and engaging and to hold the reader and audience's attention, you must organize your material (even though it's technically not a story and not fiction) as if it were a story and as if it were fiction.

94.

A NON-STORY IS A STORY

What exactly is a story?

How, one may reasonably ask, can I take my Masters' thesis on the metaphysics of motley in the works of Joseph Conrad or my Gardening Class speech on winter soil preparation for geraniums and make it into a narrative?

Trust me, you can.

Let's start by reviewing the universal principles of storytelling. (This is really a distillation of everything we've learned so far from advertising, fiction, and filmmaking.)

1) Every story must have a concept. It must put a unique and original spin, twist or framing device upon the material.

2) Every story must be about something. It must have a theme.

3) Every story must have a beginning, a middle, and an end. Act One, Act Two, Act Three.

4) Every story must have a hero.

5) Every story must have a villain.

6) Every story must start with an Inciting Incident, embedded within which is the story's climax.

7) Every story must escalate through Act Two in terms of energy, stakes, complication and significance/meaning as it progresses.

8) Every story must build to a climax centered around a clash between the hero and the villain that pays off everything that came before and that pays it off on-theme.

There is nothing about any of these principles that cannot be applied to nonfiction, including your presentation on geraniums to the Master Gardening class.

95.

A NON-STORY IS A STORY, PART TWO

Let's break these principles down into something a little more digestible.

What are the universal structural elements of all stories?

Hook.

Build.

Payoff.

This is the shape any story must take.

A beginning that grabs the listener.

A middle that escalates in tension, suspense, stakes, and excitement.

And an ending that brings it all home with a bang.

That's a novel, that's a play, that's a movie. That's a joke, that's a seduction, that's a military campaign.

It's also your TED talk, your sales pitch, your Master's thesis, and the 890-page true saga of your great-great-grandmother's life.

HOW TO WRITE
A BORING MEMOIR

Your great-great-grandmother crossed the prairie in a Conestoga wagon. You have photos of her; she looked exactly like Julia Roberts. Grandma Julia fought off bushwhackers and marauding Comanches. She gave birth on the trail. To twins. In all, she raised eleven children, buried three husbands, lived to be 106 and was twice elected mayor of Pocatello, Idaho.

Okay. Let's take this great story and screw it up royally.

1) We'll begin with Grandma Julia's birth.
2) Continue through her childhood and education.
3) Cover the Conestoga period.
4) Describe her various marriages, her child-rearing experiences, her political career.
5) End with Grandma Julia expiring in a nursing home in Mar Vista, California, surrounded by her loving family.

ZZZZZZZZ.

What have we done wrong? We told the story, right? We got every detail in there. Why are even Grandma Julia's most admiring descendants nodding off when they read our pages?

What we did wrong was we violated the rules of storytelling.

97.

APPLYING STORYTELLING PRINCIPLES TO NONFICTION

Start with theme.

Before we do anything else, let's decide what the story *is about*.

What does Grandma Julia's life *mean*?

Is her story about female empowerment? Is it about the white man's arch-crime of wiping out Native America and Native American culture? Is it something specific to Grandma Julia's family? A male-female struggle, perhaps, with a father or a husband? A great love? Is it something religious? Personal? Political?

We have to work hard here.

This is the toughest and most important part of the whole project.

Why do we want to write about this subject? What grabs us about Grandma Julia's story? Do we just want to brag about our family? Or is there some issue buried here that we believe is powerful, compelling, significant?

Find that issue.

Break it down into a single sentence.

I'll help you. Let's pick a theme arbitrarily, for purposes of illustration.

Let's say Grandma Julia's story is about Manifest Destiny. The dream of a generation to make a better life by going west.

That's good.

It's big. It has scale. It's very American, but it resonates as well with any massive, continental/historical scale epic. It could be *The Good Earth*. It could be *Reds*. It could be *Doctor Zhivago*.

Grandma Julia suffered. She lost husbands, children. She lost her youth, her beauty. She started out sweet and innocent; she ended up grizzled and tough. She prevailed. She lived to see her grandchildren settled, prosperous. But she paid a terrible price.

We're getting closer.

The story is about … what?

The human toll of a grand, visionary, national dream.

Now we're talking.

Now we've got something.

Not only have we "got something" in terms of a compelling theme for a story but, if we're right, we've just put our finger on the true significance and meaning, not only of Grandma Julia's life, but also of the lives of millions like her, in the U.S. and around the world, and not just in her era but in all times and all places.

98.

MAKE OUR HERO
EMBODY THE THEME

We've done this already without even realizing it.
We let the theme arise from Grandma Julia's story itself.

99.

CUT EVERYTHING THAT IS NOT ON-THEME

Of what remains, present it as on-theme.

When we write of Grandma Julia's young womanhood starving in Boston, after that hellish sea passage from Ireland, when we relate her suffering, the loss of her first husband killed in an outbreak of typhus, of her own brutalization at the hands of those who took advantage of immigrants … when we write of this, set it all in the context of the Westward Dream.

Julia's travails in the East serve as setup and motivation for the desperate, dangerous decision to strike out west into the unknown.

Cut everything that's not on-theme.

And what you keep, make all of it work on-theme.

100.

IDENTIFY THE CLIMAX

We're following, now, the screenwriter's axiom of "Start at the end."

What, we ask ourselves, is the climax of Grandma Julia's story? What scene or sequence does the entire saga build to? (Remember, it doesn't have to be the latest chronologically.)

Again, for illustration purposes, let's pick something arbitrarily.

A river crossing somewhere out West.

In winter.

With the Comanches attacking.

Somewhere, crossing the continent, the wagon train meets its ultimate test. An ice-choked river, enemies attacking, horses and wagons going under. Grandpa Seth (Julia's beloved second husband) is shot and scalped before her eyes. Half the wagon train is massacred. Julia herself has to sacrifice Annie, her six-year-old daughter, by letting her slip away in the river current, to save the other two boys and two girls.

In other words, a scene in which Grandma Julia pays the ultimate price a mother can pay, in the name of the Westward Dream of a better life for her family.

That's our climax.

That's the core and beating heart of Julia's story.

It's great, not just for the visceral, heartbreaking, heroic, tragic quality of the moment but also because it is dead-ass *on-theme*.

Can you see how we as writers, having decided nothing but the theme and the climax, can already tell that we've got a cracking great story?

And, even better, a story that is not just specific to Grandma Julia's personal narrative but is also universal to an entire generation and to a nation, generation after generation?

101.

SOLVE THE CLIMAX STRUCTURALLY

How can we structure Grandma Julia's story in such a way as to save this river-crossing scene for last?

Probably we can't.

The moment is too important to skip over or to hold off. We'll have to locate it in the chronological flow, probably three-quarters of the way through the memoir.

But we can use other structural techniques to bring it back at the end.

We can "play" the scene like a teaser or a flashback recurrently in Julia's memory. It can haunt her, torment her. The entire last forty years of her life can be framed as a search for self-forgiveness, for self-understanding.

Even better, we can bring Grandma Julia back to that river in real time *and make that the climax of our story.*

What if she returns, four decades after that fatal massacre, accompanied by the children of the children she saved?

A modern bridge spans the crossing now. Julia herself travels in the latest-model automobile. The sun is shining. Pretty little towns perch on both banks. (In other words, the Westward Dream has been realized.) The river crossing looks virtually unrecognizable from the way it appeared on the day of slaughter.

But in Grandma Julia's memory—and in ours, the readers'—remains the horror of that terrible hour. Julia's guilt. Her anguish. Her forty-year struggle to make peace with what she did.

She sees a road sign marking the river ford. The site is called "Comanche Crossing." Or maybe it's named after the wagon master. Or even after husband Seth, who perished there along with six-year-old Annie.

Structuring the narrative in this way gives us something even better than the massacre climax in real time. It gives us that consummate theme-defining moment *in Julia's memory.*

Notice please that we have not in this rendition violated historical fact. In truth we have been *more faithful* to the actual events, and to their spirit, than if we had simply told the story in straight chronological order.

Now, continue applying storytelling principles to the remainder of Grandma Julia's tale.

Identify a villain. (Remember, it can be inside Julia's head.)

Break the narrative into three acts, etc.

By using storytelling principles, we have not only stayed true to the real historical material, but we have identified its essence—our theme—and given universal meaning to the tale and to Grandma Julia's life.

BOOK SIX

SELF-HELP

102.

THE WRONG WAY TO WRITE A SELF-HELP BOOK

I'm not sure I would classify *The War of Art* as "self-help." But since that's the way the book seems to be thought of, let's go with it.

How do you structure a self-help book?

Here's the wrong way:

1) Introduce the thesis (first three chapters).
2) Cite examples supporting the thesis (next hundred chapters).
3) Recap and sum up what you've presented so far (last five chapters).

In other words, "Tell 'em what you're gonna tell 'em, tell 'em, then tell 'em what you've just told 'em."

There's a story about an embassy that was sent once to the ancient Spartans. The foreign envoys spoke for hours before the assembled citizens, seeking their aid. When they had finished, the Spartans declared, "We can't remember what you said at the beginning, we were confused by what you said in the middle, and by the end we were all sound asleep."

103.

THE VOICE OF AUTHORITY

If you're a woman writing a book about weight loss for women, you'd better be a size two with washboard abs and have photos of yourself prominently displayed throughout the book. Otherwise we readers will have trouble accepting you as an authority.

Authority is critical in self-help because not only is the voice almost always that of the author addressing us readers directly (as opposed to a character in fiction or a third-person author telling a story), but also because that voice is *prescribing something* to us—a new mindset, a course of action—and urging us to change our life in accordance with that prescription.

How can a voice establish authority?

1) It can come pre-loaded by reputation in the field, like Stephen King's in *On Writing* or Twyla Tharp's in *The Creative Habit*.

2) It can speak with the backing of extensive academic research, as Susan Cain did in *Quiet*.

3) It can cite its own professional or academic credentials, like Dr. Phil or Dr. Oz or Dr. Gupta.

4) Or its record of sales and success, like Tony Robbins or Eckhart Tolle.

5) The voice in self-help can establish credibility via its TV or web show, its podcast, its blog, its

YouTube channel, its number of followers on Facebook, Twitter and Instagram, or by its dominating presence in social media.

Look how much credibility a gal named K got from a single sex tape. I'm serious. In that specific field, a flash of homemade porn established authority. It set the bar.

6) The hardest and maybe the best way to establish authority is through the quality and integrity of the voice itself.

Nature cannot be tricked or cheated. She will give up to you the object of your struggles only after you have paid her price.

Here we fall back on the lessons of advertising, movies, fiction, and nonfiction.

Concept.

Theme.

Narrative device.

If you really want to hear about it, the first thing you'll probably want to know is where I was born, and what my lousy childhood was like, and how my parents were occupied and all before they had me, and all that David Copperfield kind of crap.

Done right, a voice can convey unchallengeable authority, supported by nothing but its own ring of truth.

Of all the people you will know in a lifetime, you are the only one you will never leave or lose. To the question of your life, you are the only answer.

Napoleon Hill in *Think and Grow Rich* and Jo Coudert in *Advice from a Failure* are using the same principles as J.D. Salinger did in *The Catcher in the Rye*.

104.

THE MESS THAT BECAME
THE WAR OF ART

I can brag about this one because I had nothing to do with it. All the genius was supplied by Shawn Coyne, who edited and published (and titled) the book.

I delivered to Shawn a pile of pages. The pile was about the me-against-myself battle that's fought inside the skull of any novelist. I called it *The Writer's Life*.

Shawn said, "Lemme think about this."

Then he did what any terrific editor would do.

He made that pile of pages into a story.

105.

HOW SHAWN STRUCTURED
THE WAR OF ART

What specifically did Shawn do?

First, he spread the chapters out on his floor. Then he organized them into three sections.

Hook.

Build.

Payoff.

Act One, Act Two, Act Three.

The hook, Shawn decided, was the chapters describing what I called "Resistance," i.e., the invisible negative force of self-sabotage that all writers (and creative people in all fields) face.

Why was this the Hook?

Because when the reader moved through these chapters, Shawn felt certain, she would be thinking, "OMG, I experience that same negative force when I sit down to write! Pressfield is describing *my* inner world, *my* interior struggle. I have never thought of that force as 'Resistance,' but the term rings absolutely true. *That's* the diabolical foe that's been screwing me up for years!"

The reader is hooked in this case not by a *story*, e.g., a murder mystery or a spy thriller, but by her shared experience (with me, the writer of the book) of an internal monster that has wreaked havoc on her artistic life but that until now she could never quite put her finger on.

Finishing this section (the Hook), the reader naturally wants to know more. "Where did this negative force of

Resistance come from? What is its nature? How can I fight it and overcome it?"

Shawn collated a second stack of chapters.

He thought of this as the Build.

He titled this pile, from its content, "Turning Pro." These chapters were my answer to the question, "How do we overcome Resistance?"

Do you see the story principles at work? See the book taking shape?

Act Two, i.e., the Build, mounts to a high point at which the problem has been defined and the answer has been spelled out.

Which leads inevitably to the next series of questions in the reader's mind.

"What does this all mean? Why does this negative force of Resistance exist? What is its significance in the greater scheme of things?"

Act Three.

The Payoff.

Shawn titled these chapters, "The Higher Realm."

This final section, as Shawn created it by organizing existing but scattered chapters, was where I got into deeper waters on the subject of self-sabotage. These were the "positive" chapters, the inspirational ones, because:

1) They set the phenomenon of Resistance within a wider, more cosmic context (which, to me, is a grand Miltonian battle between heaven and hell, God and Satan) that included the *positive forces* of inspiration, serendipity, self-discipline, enthusiasm, passion, and the concept of an artistic calling, all of which served to counter the negative force of Resistance.

2) They paid off the Hook and the Build by reinforcing the reader's own rising self-confidence that she had

not only identified the enemy and now knew how to fight it, but had been turned on to the unseen, unbidden, but powerfully fortifying forces that would ineluctably come to her aid once she committed to her calling and took up the challenge.

If the Hook in *The War of Art* is, "Here's the problem" …

If the Build is, "Here's the solution" …

Then the Payoff is, "Ms. Writer, your role in this timeless, epic struggle is noble, valorous, and necessary. Heed the calling of your heart. Stand and go forth."

106.

FLASHBACK: CONCEPT IN
THE WAR OF ART

Back to what we learned in advertising:
Every ad must have a concept.
And what we learned in Hollywood:
Every movie must have a concept.
In fiction:
Every novel must have a concept.
And nonfiction:
Every work of nonfiction must have a concept.
The concept in *The War of Art* is "Forget Time Management and Motivational Pep Talks and tips about How to Aim High, Persevere, and Succeed. Instead let's dig beneath everything and state straight-out what all of us know but have never dared say:

> There is an Evil Force that is constantly defeating us as artists and bringing to naught all of our dreams. Let's name that force, accept it as our enemy, and figure out how to overcome it.

107.

FLASHBACK: NARRATIVE DEVICE IN *THE WAR OF ART*

Remember our example of narrative device in *Portnoy's Complaint* and *To Kill a Mockingbird* (not to mention *Pirates of the Caribbean* and *The Martian*)?

A self-help book needs a narrative device too.

In *The War of Art,* my intention was to create a character that served as the narrative device. This character wouldn't be "me" exactly. It would be a version of me, focused entirely on sharing my own in-the-trenches experience toward the end of aiding and encouraging the reader.

A lot of thought went into defining this character.

In the end I decided:

1) The character had to talk straight.
2) He had to be as tough with the reader as I am with myself.
3) He had to establish authority via his own experience as a writer. This experience had to include enough success to be credible and enough failure to be relatable.
4) The character had to speak to the reader peer to peer. I wanted to talk as if I were addressing myself, both because I wanted to respect the reader and because I believed that this tone was the one that the reader would respect.

5) Toward that end, the character would offer no "tips" or "exercises." The issue, I believed, was too important to trivialize.

6) The character had to be totally candid, particularly about his own weaknesses and failures. Not so as to be "likeable," but to encourage the equally-fallible reader and to make him or her feel that they are not alone in their struggle.

7) The character had to truly and passionately believe in the worthiness of the artist's calling—that of all artists and all creative types—and believe with equal conviction in the supreme value of art itself.

Fortunately, that's pretty much who I am and what I believe. Once I got the rhythm and the tone, everything flowed seamlessly.

My conclusion:

Narrative device is supremely important in self-help. You, the writer, *are* the reader. The reader will hear you and listen to you only to the extent that she knows you know what you're talking about and that you are there only to help.

108.

FLASHBACK: HERO AND VILLAIN IN *THE WAR OF ART*

The War of Art is nonfiction. Like your TED talk or your presentation on geraniums, it has no characters. No story. No hero. No villain. No archetypal mentors or spirit animals. No All Is Lost moment.

Or does it?

The hero of *The War of Art* is the reader.

The villain is Resistance.

The All Is Lost moment happened in the reader's heart long before she picked up the book.

Me? I'm Obi-Wan Kenobi.

My last words to you are, "Trust the Force, Luke."

109.

SELF-HELP IS STORY

The War of Art employed all the storytelling principles of fiction and movies, as well as a number of ideas from advertising.

It had a concept and a theme. It employed three-act structure. It had a hero and a villain, a narrative device, a voice. It had an inciting incident and an All Is Lost moment and it paid off on-theme.

In other words, like other types of nonfiction, self-help can be treated as story and be conceived and structured in accord with storytelling principles.

BOOK SEVEN

THE ARTIST'S CALLING

110.

HOW CAREERS HAPPEN,
PART TWO

It happened for me from the inside out.

I was seized by an idea. I followed it. It failed.

I was seized by another idea. I followed it, and it failed too.

I did that a hundred times. Five hundred.

Finally an idea or two succeeded.

While I was thrashing from one idea to the next, I could discern no pattern. It all felt random. Each passage was one of a kind.

But when I looked back, I could see not just a pattern. I could see a career.

It had been there all along, infallibly working itself out.

111.

THERE IS A DEVIL

Resistance is real. Self-sabotage is a fact.

Radiating off the blank page, the empty canvas, the unexposed can of film is a force of relentless, merciless, protean evil that makes the Emperor Ming look like your sweet aunt Edna.

That's Reality #1.

Anyone who tells you different is a liar.

112.

THERE IS A MUSE

As powerful as is the negative, destructive force we name Resistance, so mighty is the positive, creative force we call the Muse.

Sit down. Open the faucet. The stuff that will appear, sometimes anyway, will exceed your fondest visions.

You will stare down at it and exclaim, "Where in the world did *that* come from?"

113.

JEAN-PAUL SARTRE
SCARED ME TO DEATH

I remember studying the Existentialists in high school English. Mr. Wittern (or maybe it was Mr. Lund) wrote on the blackboard:

GOD IS DEAD

EVERYTHING IS RANDOM

LIFE HAS NO MEANING

Even then I knew that was bullshit.

114.

THE ARTIST'S WORLD
IS MENTAL

The sphere of the artist is the mind.

His currency is imagination.

He asks (how can he not?), "Where do ideas come from?"

Did *Rhapsody in Blue* come to Gershwin in the shower? Was J.K. Rowling baking a pie when she first imagined Hogwarts? Or was he at the piano and she at her writing desk?

Like the monk and the mystic, the artist enters a mental space. He becomes a child. She becomes a vessel.

They tune in to the Cosmic Radio Station and listen to whatever song is being broadcast specifically to them.

115.

THE ARTIST'S SKILL

We know what a carpenter does. We can understand the work of a surgeon. But what does an artist do? Of what does her skill consist?

It's this:

The artist enters the Void with nothing and comes back with something.

Her skill is to turn off the self-censor.

Her skill is to jump off the cliff.

Her skill is to believe.

As artists, what are we believing in? We're believing in a conception of the universe (or at least of consciousness within that universe) that is not random, not pointless, not devoid of meaning.

We're believing in a mental reality that is active, creative, self-organizing, self-perpetuating, infinitely diverse and yet cohesive, governed by laws that are not beyond the grasp and ken of human understanding.

We're believing that the universe has a gift that it is holding *specifically for us* and that, if we can learn to make ourselves available to it, it will deliver this gift into our hands.

Believe me, this is true.

116.

ARE YOU A WRITER?

I always wanted to be a writer. For years, decades even, I could not apply that term to myself. I did not consider myself worthy.

I was trying to be a writer.

I was aspiring to be a writer.

But I was not a writer.

I'm not even sure what I meant by that term. Was it some exalted station, like "fighter pilot" or "Zen monk?" I still can't say.

But I am a writer now.

I have paid my dues. I have earned my wings. Maybe I'm not a great writer or even a good one, but I *am* a writer.

I wanted it and, for good or ill, I have made it come true.

117.

THE WHITE WHALE

The #1 question that writers ask themselves: "I've got a million ideas. How do I know which one to work on?"

Answer: Write your White Whale.

Which idea, of all those swimming inside your brain, are you compelled to pursue the way Ahab was driven to hunt Moby Dick?

Here's how you know—you're scared to death of it.

It's good to be scared. You should be scared. Mediocre ideas never elevate the heart rate. Great ones make you break out in a sweat.

The final image of *Moby Dick* is one of the most powerful and compelling ever, not just as the climax to a story, an adventure, a tragedy, but as a metaphor for the artist's calling and his endlessly-repeated, never-ending struggle. Do you remember the scene?

(Actually this is from the movie, written by Ray Bradbury, which I think took Melville one better.)

Ahab has chased Moby Dick around the Horn and across all the oceans of the globe. At last he has closed with the leviathan, sunk his harpoon into the great beast. But in the clash of whale and whaling boat, Ahab has been snarled in the harpoon lines and pulled over the side …

He is lashed now, bodily, to the White Whale—so entangled in the ropes that he cannot get free. Ahab can see Moby Dick's eye, and the whale can see him. Clearly the monster recognizes his tormenter; in moments he will sound, dragging Ahab down hundreds of feet into the ocean's depths.

Ahab knows this. He knows that his obsessive pursuit has led inexorably to his own extinction. But that awareness does nothing to abate his fury. Clutching the harpoon in both hands, he plunges its steel lance head again and again into the flesh of this creature he hates but can never kill.

AHAB

Towards thee I roll, thou all-destroying but unconquering whale; to the last I grapple with thee; from hell's heart I stab at thee; for hate's sake I spit my last breath at thee!

That's the writer's life in a nutshell.

But I would invert Melville's concept. I don't think you hate the whale.

I think you love it.

The whale is your unwritten book, your unsung song, your calling as an artist. You die grappling with this thing, lashed to it, battling it even as it takes you under.

But your death is not a mortal death. You die instead the artist's death, which leads to resurrection in a higher, nobler form and recruits you to the next hunt, the next chase, the pursuit of the next Thing You Love.

Is there a White Whale out there for you? There is or you wouldn't be reading this book.

You'll know that whale by these qualities:

Its accomplishment will seem beyond your resources. Your pursuit of it will bear you into waters where no one before you has sailed. To hunt this beast will require everything you've got.

You may have started, like me, as a junior Mad Man, scripting jingles for canine kibble. There's nothing wrong with that. You may have prostituted your talent, sold out to the Man. I have, a thousand times.

It doesn't matter. I forgive you and I forgive myself. Each incarnation is an apprenticeship, if you live it that way.

Are you slaving now in some sell-out job? Are you living a Shadow Career instead of your real calling?

It's okay. It's all part of the journey.

What you learn in Wrong Career #1 will serve you in Off-Key Career #2 and in Out-of-Kilter Career #3, and the wisdom you acquire in #1, #2, and #3 will form the foundation of Real Calling #4 (or #5 or #6 or however long it takes.)

118.

NOBODY WANTS TO
READ YOUR SH*T

What Nobody Wants to Read Your Shit means is that none of us wants to hear your self-centered, ego-driven, unrefined demands for attention. Why should we? It's boring. There's nothing in it for us.

Can you sing the blues? Can you make a shoe? Make it beautiful. Make it fun and sexy and interesting and I'll buy it. I'll wear it. I'll tell my friends about it. Your book, your poem, your movie can even be despairing, as long as it's profoundly conceived and takes my understanding of life a little bit deeper.

What Nobody Wants to Read Your Shit means is that you/we/all of us as writers must learn to leave space for the reader, to work our offerings like a miner refines ore, until what comes out on the page is solid, glistening gold.

If it's our soul that we're talking about (rather than just What We Write), then our passage through the varying disciplines of this life, if we're truly paying attention, is an education in editing out the ego, in stepping away from our fear and self-concern and aspirations for recognition, for material rewards, and for earthly payoffs, until we move into the realm of the gift, where what we offer is for the reader's good and not our own.

Want me to read your shit? Do that and I will.

APPENDIX

And our final literary field...

BOOK EIGHT

PORN

119.

SEX SCENES

Ionce did a rewrite on a skin flick. Before he would let me begin, the producer wanted to meet for breakfast, to give me my marching orders and to make sure that I didn't slow the project down by making any rookie mistakes. (Who knew how to tweak a porno film?)

We met at a coffee shop in Santa Monica. In that meeting, I got two of the best lessons in writing I've ever received.

The first thing the producer said was that he hated virtually every porn movie he'd ever seen. They were all, he said, so lame and predictable.

"Every one is the same: talk, talk, screw, screw. That's why they're so lousy. That's not good storytelling. Here's what I want from you—when you get to a sex scene, don't let the story come to a screeching halt while we watch two people bang each other."

Wow, I thought, that's pretty smart.

"Make the screwing scene advance the story," the producer said. "Wherever the story stands when the actors start to jump each other's bones, I want it to have moved to the next level by the time they finish."

He gave me an example. "Let's say the characters are a private eye and his gorgeous client. They hop into bed. By the time they climb out, I want the story to have advanced to a new stage. She spills something about the crime, he reveals some secret from his past, whatever. Make the story 'turn' and mount to a higher level."

I confess I had gone into this meeting expecting the worst—and even condescending in my mind both to the producer and to the project. Suddenly the scales fell from my eyes. My employer had become a mentor! Immediately I grasped that the don't-stop-the-story principle could be applied to other, more mainstream genres.

Action movies. How many car chases, I was thinking, have I seen where the story comes to a dead stop while we watch Ford Mustangs crash and eighteen-wheel tanker trucks explode? (In fact I was working on an action movie at that very time and I was making that exact mistake.) Note to self: Rewrite that fist fight and *make the story turn.*

Musicals. Every song should advance the story.

Flashbacks. Every digression must bring in something new that propels the narrative forward.

"Okay, kid, that's Point #1. Got it? Now here's the second issue. Never write me a sex scene where nothing happens but the sex. Always have something else going on at the same time.

"Let's say the wife is getting it on in the bedroom with the horny carpenter. Now the husband comes home unannounced. He enters the front door. The husband doesn't know the wife and the carpenter are in the bedroom. The wife and the carpenter don't know the husband has just come in the front door. Now we've got something! When we edit the film, we can cut back and forth and milk the suspense. It's not just two people screwing, see? We've added a second dimension. And when the husband discovers what his old lady's up to, we've advanced the story!"

Holy cow, another bulls-eye! This second principle,

I could see, could also be applied to all kinds of situations in mainstream features.

Wow.

And I was getting paid for this!

I went home and rewrote the script, following the producer's principles scrupulously. It worked. I was amazed at how much better the screenplay got.

In the end, alas, the movie never got made. The financing fell through. And I (no surprise) never got paid. I didn't care. I had learned something. I had advanced my command of the craft.

A couple of years later, I was having dinner at a different restaurant when I saw the producer come in with his wife and two young kids. It would make a more colorful story if I could describe him as a cigar-chomping Tinseltown philistine, but in fact he was a sweet guy and a regular family man. I wanted to thank him for what he had taught me. I had put it to use, over and over, on other, non-X-rated projects. But I thought, seeing him with his children in tow, that maybe discretion was the better part of valor. I exited without going out of my way to catch his eye.

But thanks, Andy. I learned more about storytelling from you in half an hour than I would have in four years at the Yale Drama School.

Made in United States
Orlando, FL
22 February 2024

44015314R00114